Four Column INVENTORY Forms Only

Steps 4 & 10

Pan Fellowship

© Copyright 2008 by HP Publishing (UK) Ltd
63 Shepherds Court
LONDON W12-8PW
England

44+(0)208 740 8567
www.hppublishing.com
www.hpretreats.org

First Edition

This edition was printed in the United Kingdom

ISBN 978-0-9556930-5-2

Chapter 1

How to Answer Fourth Column Questions

HOW DO WE ANSWER SUCH QUESTIONS; AS?

- *"Where had we been selfish, self-centred or self-seeking?"*
- *"Where had we been dishonest?"*
- *"Where had we been frightened?"*
- *"Where had we been* (responsible) *to blame?"*
- *"What decisions did we make based on self that later placed us in a position to be hurt?"*
- *"When in the past can we remember making this decision?"*
- *"Where were we wrong? What was our part?"*

The more we work with people in these various programs the more we realise how very difficult it is to begin to look at life's situations from a whole new angle. Many of our sponsees look at us with blank stares when asked questions such as those above.

These are difficult questions. Most of us think that we are anything but selfish, dishonest, and are really victims to life's deranged sense of humour. But taking them one at a time, let's see if we just might be the architects of our own life. And if we are; can we reconstruct our lives?

- *"Where had we been selfish, self-centred or self-seeking?"*

Below we find a list of attitudes that may just suggest ways in which we might possibly be "selfish, self-centred or self-seeking." The most important trait to become aware of is that consideration of others, or other opinions, is not usually our first reaction.

HOW TO ANSWER...

SELFISH/SELF CENTRED —	SELF-SEEKING
• Wanting things our way	• Being possessive
• Wanting special treatment	• Thinking we're better
• Wanting our "needs" met	• Thinking others are jealous
• Wanting what others have	• Reacting from self-loathing
• Wanting control	• Reacting self-righteously
• Wanting to be the best	• Too concerned about me
• Wanting others to be like me	• Manipulating others to our will
• Wanting more than my share	• Putting others down to build us up (internally or externally)
• Wanting to look good at another's expense	• Engaging in character assassination
• Wanting to be liked	• Acting superior
• Not seeing others' POV	• Acting out to fill a void
• Not seeing others' problems	• Engaging in gluttony
• Not seeing others' "needs"	• Lusting after another
• Not being a friend	• Ignoring others' needs
• Being dependant	• Trying to control others
• Being dominant	• Getting revenge when I don't get my way
• Being grandiose	• Acting out to feel good
• Being miserly	• Simply holding a resentment

"**Where had we been dishonest?**"

Dishonesty covers much more than just "cheque book" honesty. There are many ways in which we lie to ourselves and others, both overtly and covertly. **"Life is a totality, and...it can't be compartmentalised. Dishonesty in one area creates problems in another area. Healing in one segment provides better health in another. It is all connected. Each Step blends with another in an integrated, comprehensive programme designed to transform you and me into human beings capable of willingly and joyously doing God's will."** [1]

"*Doc* (Dr. Bob)...*was pretty positive that God's law was the Law of Love and that all my resentful feelings which I had fed and cultivated...were the result of either conscious or unconscious, it didn't matter which, disobedience to that law...*

"*Taking love as the basic command I discovered that my faithful attempt to practice a law of love led me to clear myself of*

FOURTH COLUMN QUESTIONS

certain dishonesties." [2] These dishonesties we find in ourselves as well as others. We cannot fool ourselves about honesty as this woman did during her inventory process. **"The questions he asked me that I didn't answer honestly, I thought were none of his business."**[3] We justify our lies mainly by fooling ourselves that it is the right thing to do.

DISHONEST

- Not seeing/admitting where we were at fault
- Having a superior attitude
- Thinking we're better
- Blaming others for our problems
- Not admitting we've done the same thing
- Not expressing feelings
- Not expressing ideas
- Not being clear
- Hiding our true motives
- Lying
- Cheating
- Stealing
- Not facing facts
- Hiding from reality
- Holding on to false beliefs
- Breaking rules or laws
- Lying to ourselves
- Exaggerating
- Minimising
- Setting ourselves up to be "wronged"
- Expecting others to be what they're not
- Being a perfectionist

"Where had we been frightened?"

As it says earlier, **"fear is an evil and corroding thread"** that distorts and harms our lives. Psychology has demonstrated that humans are only born with two fears; fear of loud noises and fear of loss of physical support. Therefore all other fears are not natural. Could these fears be where our defiance comes from? **"I was as defiant as anybody could be because I was scared."**[4] Let us look at just a few of those "unnatural" fears.

FEARS

- Of peoples' opinions
- Of rejection
- Of abandonment
- Of loneliness
- Of physical injury
- Of abuse
- Of not being able to change ourselves or others
- Of not being in control
- Of our inferiority
- Of our inadequacy
- Of criticism
- Of expressing our feelings
- Of expressing our ideas
- Of getting trapped
- Of exposure
- Of embarrassment

FORMS ONLY

HOW TO ANSWER...
"WHERE HAD WE BEEN (RESPONSIBLE) TO BLAME?"

"All my life I had blamed everything that ever happened to me on someone else, and I usually could find someone." [5] As we outlined earlier in a footnote the word *responsible* could be broken down into two words: **response** and **able**. So the word can be interpreted to mean: *"What **response** are we **able** to give to any situation?"* and for that we are responsible.

In the following exercise we will look at our response to what has happened in our lives and the results of those responses. We are looking for the lost power in our lives. By realising that it is not what has happened to us but how we reacted to those events that has defined our lives, we recognise that we can change our reactions. The goal is to have the events of our past be just that, past events and not remain decisive factors in our present. Very often we felt compelled to make these decisions or choices at an early age, when our reason was under-developed.

Most of us wouldn't ask a child for advice on how to deal with a complex emotional or spiritual dilemma. But isn't that what we have done? This has determined the very lives that we live today. All based on a child's decisions and choices? As a result we find ourselves living with emotional insecurity. The **"Common symptoms of emotional insecurity are worry, anger, self-pity and depression."** [6] Who among us would not want to rid ourselves of this emotional baggage?

Uncovering our imperfections and flaws, discovering where **we** are responsible and discarding these errors is a lifetime process. If we work the programme each day, every tomorrow gets better and better. Becoming a better human being is wonderful but it is not our final destination. It is just a step toward the purpose for which we were born. We were not born to cry, to strive, to struggle. We have lost our way, like the prodigal son. We were born in the image and likeness of an Intelligent Universe. The purpose of our life is to return to our Creator in that intelligent image and likeness; to see this **"Great Reality"** as our presence, our soul, our very being, and let It live our life for us, as us.

Our character defects have been passed down from generation to generation. While we are not to blame for inheriting these shortcomings, we are *responsible* for their continued use. Every thought, action, word, and deed is recorded in Universal Consciousness and, like radio waves, connects with those who are receptive. From birth these defects cause us to make mistakes over and over again with every one we come in contact with. They are impersonal; logged in our

FOURTH COLUMN QUESTIONS

memory. When a situation arises we sort through past experiences, often unconsciously, to work out how to handle it. It's all we know. If in our past experiences we became angry, violent and yelled; or became passive and weak then that's how we react now. If it was to lie, we lie; if we were grovelling, we grovel. It is impersonal. We are not to blame.

The most important thing for us to get from this question is that we are responsible for:

1. ***Our emotions***—our feelings
2. ***Our actions*** and reactions
3. ***Our beliefs,*** stemming from our thinking—decisions and choices

BLAME (RESPONSIBLE)

- For harsh judgement
- For ignoring the facts
- Being careless
- Bringing the past into the present
- Not dealing with our feelings
- Blaming others for our feelings
- Not working our programme
- For our own upset
- For our ignorance

"WHAT DECISIONS DID WE MAKE BASED ON SELF THAT LATER PLACED US IN A POSITION TO BE HURT?"

"When in the past can we remember making this decision?"

In order to understand the decisions we have made in these situations, we should understand how the human mind works. What follows is an over-simplified explanation of the mental process involved. The human mind makes a decision or choice based on what it perceives as necessary for its survival. Once this judgment has been made, our mind then gathers evidence to prove to itself that it has made the right decision. Our mind never gathers evidence to prove it's wrong or even take into account facts that may suggest it's not right. Unless of course by proving that we are wrong again, is evidence of us being right about always being wrong. This is where everything could get very complicated. For this work let's "Keep it Simple": **Our mind never thinks it's wrong.**

The ultimate aim of our continuing inventory is to recognise and transform these past choices and decisions and replace them with reasonable ones. These choices and decisions are what have created

HOW TO ANSWER...

our beliefs in life; not what actually happened to us but what we made what happened mean. Regaining "Power" in our lives is accomplished by this recognition and the changing of these old decisions and choices; and therefore our beliefs. Then we find those beliefs are supported by the Universe just as our past beliefs have always been. As she looked back on her life, this woman said, **"Slowly, my life seemed to unfold before me, shedding insights on childhood resentments, jealousies, and fears that had mushroomed in adulthood."** [7]

On this subject of decisions or choices let us look at a few other things that can assist us in our quest for freedom. In early childhood we tend to watch our parents very closely, it doesn't seem to matter much whether we like who they are or not. Our choices as to who we emulate are usually based on who seemed to get their way. Who appeared to get what they wanted? This is why those of us who have had a bullying parent, even though we hated the way they were, end up being bullies ourselves. Or, when we have had what seemed to be a weak and whiney victim as one of our parents who in the end seems to get their way, we adopt the role of victim in life. Often our personalities are parts of both personality traits.

When taking the kind of look at our lives that this programme requires, we see that when establishing the very foundation of our lives we were *given choice* over our response to everything. This is what mystics (men who have walked in enlightenment) have been trying to tell us for millennia. At this stage of the Steps we resemble the Prodigal Son in the biblical story, who returned home and was presented with a ring and a cloak, symbols of maturity and responsibility. Likewise, when we make conscious connection to the presence of a Higher Power and take full responsibility for our own lives and actions, we become responsible, and therefore really free, adults.

Whatever we trusted and believed in yesterday we have become today. Whatever we trust and believe in today becomes our tomorrow. This is the miracle of the programme. We are no longer shackled by our past unconscious beliefs and behaviour patterns. Through exercising free choice today, we reshape our tomorrows. One day at a time.

The beliefs that we have held onto that do not serve us well we can, through inventory, discard. If we do not inventory them, and therefore find that they have no value, we are doomed to repeat these past beliefs again and again. We are surely free to do so, we are not automatons. If we truly desire a new life we *must* see that the things that we thought were good for us are not always so. The reason is that we are using the same old information locked in the memory banks of our minds. A human mind, that is weighing and measuring what is

FOURTH COLUMN QUESTIONS

best for its destiny, is waging a losing proposition. We only have to look at our lives up till now to see that our unaided judgement is flawed. Uncovering our past mistakes, discovering where **we** made the decisions and choices that truly harmed us, and discarding these errors is a lifetime practice.

What about our "geographic cures" for our problems? When things got too bad ***"I moved away. I never thought about changing myself, I always thought about changing people, or changing places."***[8]

We are all trying to win at this game of life. What we learn in the programme is that we can only truly win when we create positive, loving attitudes towards life itself. Napoleon Hill once wrote: ***"what ever the mind... can conceive and believe it can achieve."***[9] We lay particular emphasis on this part of the process acknowledged recently by us, as part of the inventory process. Yet it has always been there: ***"we invariably find that in the past we have made decisions based on self which later placed us in a position to be hurt."***[10] Finally, the decisions that most affect us are those generalised ones that colour our overall beliefs about people, places and things.

So, what is the underlying personality characteristic of those of us with addictive personalities? Well ***"a number of eminent psychologists and doctors made an exhaustive study of a good-sized group... The doctors weren't trying to find out how different we were from one another; they sought to find whatever personality traits, if any, this group...had in common. These distinguished men had the nerve to say that most...under investigation were still childish, emotionally sensitive, and grandiose."***[11] This implies that up till now our most defining decisions were made by ***"childish, emotionally sensitive, and grandiose"*** sides of ourselves. What a kettle of fish that is, no wonder our lives are such a mess.

HOW TO ANSWER...

DECISIONS

- People are stupid
- Women are weak
- Women are dangerous
- Women are ...
- Men are better off
- Men are liars
- Men are ...
- We can't trust women
- We can't trust men
- I am stupid
- I am always right
- I am always wrong
- Nobody loves me
- I'm unlovable
- I'm ugly
- I have a bad temper
- My nose is too big
- Sex is dirty
- Marriage is ...
- Life is ...
- Heights are...
- Bugs are ...
- Pets are ...
- Whites are ...
- Blacks are ...
- Spanish are ...
- Germans are ...
- Americans are ...
- British are ...
- French are ...
- Etc. etc. etc.

"WHERE WERE WE WRONG—WHAT WAS OUR PART?"

Admitting that we are wrong is very difficult for many of us. But we have all made mistakes, a lot of them. Besides for our purposes wrong simple means mistaken. Our part is often found after reviewing the answers to the above questions. What we are looking for here is that part for which we are responsible. That part that if we had not perpetrated, the damage to our present lives could not have happened.

OUR PART

- Gathering evidence to prove ourselves right
- Making sweeping generalisations
- The rest of our part will be a distillation of the answers to the preceding questions

Some of us use what we have learned in the programme to look at what others aren't doing; this is **"known as 'taking someone else's inventory,' a practice at which...** (We) **can be expert."** [12] But we find this practice to be a fruitless one.

The way to reach God and freedom is through a thorough self-survey. This is done by taking every disturbing defect, resentment, fear, financial and sex problem of our memory, and seeing where the problem and disinformation started. Finding out what decisions or choices we made and where we deceived and deluded ourselves. This is our chosen path of freedom.

FOUR COLUMN INVENTORY...

Chapter 2

Inventory Forms
...Column Work

COLUMN WORK

Resentment (1) and/or Fear:	The Cause (Column 2)	Affects Our: (Column 3)
Person, Place or Thing		☐ Self-Esteem ☐ Security ☐ Ambitions ☐ Personal Relations ☐ Sex Relations ☐ Pride/Shame ☐ Fear
Ask Ourselves: ** (AA 67.3) * (AA 62.2)	Putting out of our mind the wrong others had done, we resolutely looked for our own mistakes… We admitted our wrongs honestly…** **STEPS 4 and/or 10 - (Column 4)**	
Where had I been selfish, self-centred or self-seeking?**		
Where had I been dishonest?**		
Where had I been frightened?**		
For what had I been responsible?**		
What decisions did I make based on self that later placed me in a position to be hurt?*		
When in the past did I make this decision? * (Earliest memory)		
Where was I wrong,** what was my part?		
STEPS 6 & 7 – List of Character Defects		
---	---	---	---	---

STEP 9 - Amends	STEP 8
	☐ Now ☐ Later ☐ Never

FOUR COLUMN INVENTORY…FORMS ONLY

INVENTORY FORMS

Resentment (1) and/or Fear:	The Cause (Column 2)	Affects Our: (Column 3)
Person, Place or Thing		☐ Self-Esteem ☐ Security ☐ Ambitions ☐ Personal Relations ☐ Sex Relations ☐ Pride/Shame ☐ Fear
Ask Ourselves: ** (AA 67.3) * (AA 62.2)	Putting out of our mind the wrong others had done, we resolutely looked for our own mistakes… We admitted our wrongs honestly…** **STEPS 4** and/or **10** - **(Column 4)**	
Where had I been selfish, self-centred or self-seeking?**		
Where had I been dishonest?**		
Where had I been frightened?**		
For what had I been responsible?**		
What decisions did I make based on self that later placed me in a position to be hurt?*		
When in the past did I make this decision? * (Earliest memory)		
Where was I wrong,** what was my part?		

STEPS 6 & 7 – List of Character Defects			

STEP 9 - Amends		STEP 8	
		☐	Now
		☐	Later
		☐	Never

FOUR COLUMN INVENTORY…

COLUMN WORK

Resentment (1) and/or Fear:	The Cause (Column 2)	Affects Our: (Column 3)
Person, Place or Thing		☐ Self-Esteem ☐ Security ☐ Ambitions ☐ Personal Relations ☐ Sex Relations ☐ Pride/Shame ☐ Fear
Ask Ourselves: ** (AA 67.3) * (AA 62.2)	Putting out of our mind the wrong others had done, we resolutely looked for our own mistakes… We admitted our wrongs honestly…** **STEPS 4 and/or 10 - (Column 4)**	
Where had I been selfish, self-centred or self-seeking?**		
Where had I been dishonest?**		
Where had I been frightened?**		
For what had I been responsible?**		
What decisions did I make based on self that later placed me in a position to be hurt?*		
When in the past did I make this decision? * (Earliest memory)		
Where was I wrong,** what was my part?		

STEPS 6 & 7 – List of Character Defects			

STEP 9 - Amends	STEP 8
	☐ Now ☐ Later ☐ Never

FORMS ONLY

INVENTORY FORMS

Resentment (1) and/or Fear:	The Cause (Column 2)	Affects Our: (Column 3)
Person, Place or Thing		☐ Self-Esteem ☐ Security ☐ Ambitions ☐ Personal Relations ☐ Sex Relations ☐ Pride/Shame ☐ Fear
Ask Ourselves: ** (AA 67.3) * (AA 62.2)	Putting out of our mind the wrong others had done, we resolutely looked for our own mistakes… We admitted our wrongs honestly…** **STEPS 4** and/or **10** - **(Column 4)**	
Where had I been selfish, self-centred or self-seeking?**		
Where had I been dishonest?**		
Where had I been frightened?**		
For what had I been responsible?**		
What decisions did I make based on self that later placed me in a position to be hurt?*		
When in the past did I make this decision? * (Earliest memory)		
Where was I wrong,** what was my part?		
STEPS 6 & 7 – List of Character Defects					
STEP 9 - Amends			**STEP 8**
			☐ Now ☐ Later ☐ Never

FOUR COLUMN INVENTORY…

COLUMN WORK

Resentment (1) and/or Fear:	The Cause (Column 2)	Affects Our: (Column 3)
Person, Place or Thing		☐ Self-Esteem ☐ Security ☐ Ambitions ☐ Personal Relations ☐ Sex Relations ☐ Pride/Shame ☐ Fear
Ask Ourselves: ** (AA 67.3) * (AA 62.2)	Putting out of our mind the wrong others had done, we resolutely looked for our own mistakes… We admitted our wrongs honestly…** **STEPS 4** and/or **10** - **(Column 4)**	
Where had I been selfish, self-centred or self-seeking?**		
Where had I been dishonest?**		
Where had I been frightened?**		
For what had I been responsible?**		
What decisions did I make based on self that later placed me in a position to be hurt?*		
When in the past did I make this decision? * (Earliest memory)		
Where was I wrong,** what was my part?		
STEPS 6 & 7 – List of Character Defects		

STEP 9 - Amends	STEP 8
	☐ Now ☐ Later ☐ Never

INVENTORY FORMS

Resentment (1) and/or Fear:	The Cause (Column 2)	Affects Our: (Column 3)
Person, Place or Thing		☐ Self-Esteem ☐ Security ☐ Ambitions ☐ Personal Relations ☐ Sex Relations ☐ Pride/Shame ☐ Fear
Ask Ourselves: ** (AA 67.3) * (AA 62.2)	Putting out of our mind the wrong others had done, we resolutely looked for our own mistakes... We admitted our wrongs honestly...** **STEPS 4 and/or 10 - (Column 4)**	
Where had I been selfish, self-centred or self-seeking?**		
Where had I been dishonest?**		
Where had I been frightened?**		
For what had I been responsible?**		
What decisions did I make based on self that later placed me in a position to be hurt?*		
When in the past did I make this decision? * (Earliest memory)		
Where was I wrong,** what was my part?		
STEPS 6 & 7 – List of Character Defects		

STEP 9 - Amends	STEP 8
	☐ Now ☐ Later ☐ Never

FOUR COLUMN INVENTORY...

COLUMN WORK

Resentment (1) and/or Fear:	The Cause (Column 2)	Affects Our: (Column 3)
Person, Place or Thing		☐ Self-Esteem ☐ Security ☐ Ambitions ☐ Personal Relations ☐ Sex Relations ☐ Pride/Shame ☐ Fear
Ask Ourselves: ** (AA 67.3) * (AA 62.2)	Putting out of our mind the wrong others had done, we resolutely looked for our own mistakes… We admitted our wrongs honestly…** **STEPS 4 and/or 10 - (Column 4)**	
Where had I been selfish, self-centred or self-seeking?**		
Where had I been dishonest?**		
Where had I been frightened?**		
For what had I been responsible?**		
What decisions did I make based on self that later placed me in a position to be hurt?*		
When in the past did I make this decision? * (Earliest memory)		
Where was I wrong,** what was my part?		

STEPS 6 & 7 – List of Character Defects

STEP 9 - Amends	STEP 8
	☐ Now ☐ Later ☐ Never

FORMS ONLY

INVENTORY FORMS

Resentment (1) and/or Fear:	The Cause (Column 2)	Affects Our: (Column 3)
Person, Place or Thing		☐ Self-Esteem ☐ Security ☐ Ambitions ☐ Personal Relations ☐ Sex Relations ☐ Pride/Shame ☐ Fear
Ask Ourselves: ** (AA 67.3) * (AA 62.2)	Putting out of our mind the wrong others had done, we resolutely looked for our own mistakes... We admitted our wrongs honestly...** **STEPS 4** and/or **10 - (Column 4)**	
Where had I been selfish, self-centred or self-seeking?**		
Where had I been dishonest?**		
Where had I been frightened?**		
For what had I been responsible?**		
What decisions did I make based on self that later placed me in a position to be hurt?*		
When in the past did I make this decision? * (Earliest memory)		
Where was I wrong,** what was my part?		

STEPS 6 & 7 – List of Character Defects			

STEP 9 - Amends	STEP 8
	☐ Now ☐ Later ☐ Never

COLUMN WORK

Resentment (1) and/or Fear:	The Cause (Column 2)	Affects Our: (Column 3)
Person, Place or Thing		☐ Self-Esteem ☐ Security ☐ Ambitions ☐ Personal Relations ☐ Sex Relations ☐ Pride/Shame ☐ Fear
Ask Ourselves: ** (AA 67.3) * (AA 62.2)	Putting out of our mind the wrong others had done, we resolutely looked for our own mistakes… We admitted our wrongs honestly…** **STEPS 4 and/or 10 - (Column 4)**	
Where had I been selfish, self-centred or self-seeking?**		
Where had I been dishonest?**		
Where had I been frightened?**		
For what had I been responsible?**		
What decisions did I make based on self that later placed me in a position to be hurt?*		
When in the past did I make this decision? * (Earliest memory)		
Where was I wrong,** what was my part?		

STEPS 6 & 7 – List of Character Defects				

STEP 9 - Amends	STEP 8
	☐ Now ☐ Later ☐ Never

FORMS ONLY

INVENTORY FORMS

Resentment (1) and/or Fear:	The Cause (Column 2)	Affects Our: (Column 3)
Person, Place or Thing		☐ Self-Esteem ☐ Security ☐ Ambitions ☐ Personal Relations ☐ Sex Relations ☐ Pride/Shame ☐ Fear
Ask Ourselves: ** (AA 67.3) * (AA 62.2)	Putting out of our mind the wrong others had done, we resolutely looked for our own mistakes… We admitted our wrongs honestly…** **STEPS 4** and/or **10** - **(Column 4)**	
Where had I been selfish, self-centred or self-seeking?**		
Where had I been dishonest?**		
Where had I been frightened?**		
For what had I been responsible?**		
What decisions did I make based on self that later placed me in a position to be hurt?*		
When in the past did I make this decision? * (Earliest memory)		
Where was I wrong,** what was my part?		

STEPS 6 & 7 – List of Character Defects				

STEP 9 - Amends	STEP 8
	☐ Now ☐ Later ☐ Never

FOUR COLUMN INVENTORY…

COLUMN WORK

Resentment (1) and/or Fear:	The Cause (Column 2)	Affects Our: (Column 3)
Person, Place or Thing		☐ Self-Esteem ☐ Security ☐ Ambitions ☐ Personal Relations ☐ Sex Relations ☐ Pride/Shame ☐ Fear
Ask Ourselves: ** (AA 67.3) * (AA 62.2)	Putting out of our mind the wrong others had done, we resolutely looked for our own mistakes… We admitted our wrongs honestly…** **STEPS 4 and/or 10 - (Column 4)**	
Where had I been selfish, self-centred or self-seeking?**		
Where had I been dishonest?**		
Where had I been frightened?**		
For what had I been responsible?**		
What decisions did I make based on self that later placed me in a position to be hurt?*		
When in the past did I make this decision? * (Earliest memory)		
Where was I wrong,** what was my part?		

STEPS 6 & 7 – List of Character Defects			

STEP 9 - Amends	STEP 8
	☐ Now ☐ Later ☐ Never

FORMS ONLY

INVENTORY FORMS

Resentment (1) and/or Fear:	The Cause (Column 2)	Affects Our: (Column 3)
Person, Place or Thing		☐ Self-Esteem ☐ Security ☐ Ambitions ☐ Personal Relations ☐ Sex Relations ☐ Pride/Shame ☐ Fear
Ask Ourselves: ** (AA 67.3) * (AA 62.2)	Putting out of our mind the wrong others had done, we resolutely looked for our own mistakes... We admitted our wrongs honestly...** **STEPS 4** and/or **10** - **(Column 4)**	
Where had I been selfish, self-centred or self-seeking?**		
Where had I been dishonest?**		
Where had I been frightened?**		
For what had I been responsible?**		
What decisions did I make based on self that later placed me in a position to be hurt?*		
When in the past did I make this decision? * (Earliest memory)		
Where was I wrong,** what was my part?		

STEPS 6 & 7 – List of Character Defects			

STEP 9 - Amends	STEP 8
	☐ Now ☐ Later ☐ Never

COLUMN WORK

Resentment (1) and/or Fear:	The Cause (Column 2)	Affects Our: (Column 3)
Person, Place or Thing		☐ Self-Esteem ☐ Security ☐ Ambitions ☐ Personal Relations ☐ Sex Relations ☐ Pride/Shame ☐ Fear
Ask Ourselves: ** (AA 67.3) * (AA 62.2)	Putting out of our mind the wrong others had done, we resolutely looked for our own mistakes... We admitted our wrongs honestly... ** **STEPS 4 and/or 10 - (Column 4)**	
Where had I been selfish, self-centred or self-seeking?**		
Where had I been dishonest?**		
Where had I been frightened?**		
For what had I been responsible?**		
What decisions did I make based on self that later placed me in a position to be hurt?*		
When in the past did I make this decision? * (Earliest memory)		
Where was I wrong,** what was my part?		

STEPS 6 & 7 – List of Character Defects				

STEP 9 - Amends	STEP 8
	☐ Now ☐ Later ☐ Never

FORMS ONLY

INVENTORY FORMS

Resentment (1) and/or Fear:	The Cause (Column 2)	Affects Our: (Column 3)
Person, Place or Thing		☐ Self-Esteem ☐ Security ☐ Ambitions ☐ Personal Relations ☐ Sex Relations ☐ Pride/Shame ☐ Fear
Ask Ourselves: ** (AA 67.3) * (AA 62.2)	Putting out of our mind the wrong others had done, we resolutely looked for our own mistakes... We admitted our wrongs honestly...** **STEPS 4** and/or **10 - (Column 4)**	
Where had I been selfish, self-centred or self-seeking?**		
Where had I been dishonest?**		
Where had I been frightened?**		
For what had I been responsible?**		
What decisions did I make based on self that later placed me in a position to be hurt?*		
When in the past did I make this decision? * (Earliest memory)		
Where was I wrong,** what was my part?		
STEPS 6 & 7 – List of Character Defects			
STEP 9 - Amends		**STEP 8**
		☐ Now ☐ Later ☐ Never

FOUR COLUMN INVENTORY...

COLUMN WORK

Resentment (1) and/or Fear:	The Cause (Column 2)	Affects Our: (Column 3)
Person, Place or Thing		☐ Self-Esteem ☐ Security ☐ Ambitions ☐ Personal Relations ☐ Sex Relations ☐ Pride/Shame ☐ Fear
Ask Ourselves: ** (AA 67.3) * (AA 62.2)	Putting out of our mind the wrong others had done, we resolutely looked for our own mistakes... We admitted our wrongs honestly... ** **STEPS 4 and/or 10 - (Column 4)**	
Where had I been selfish, self-centred or self-seeking?**		
Where had I been dishonest?**		
Where had I been frightened?**		
For what had I been responsible?**		
What decisions did I make based on self that later placed me in a position to be hurt?*		
When in the past did I make this decision? * (Earliest memory)		
Where was I wrong,** what was my part?		

STEPS 6 & 7 – List of Character Defects

STEP 9 - Amends	STEP 8
	☐ Now ☐ Later ☐ Never

FORMS ONLY

INVENTORY FORMS

Resentment (1) and/or Fear:	The Cause (Column 2)	Affects Our: (Column 3)
Person, Place or Thing		☐ Self-Esteem ☐ Security ☐ Ambitions ☐ Personal Relations ☐ Sex Relations ☐ Pride/Shame ☐ Fear
Ask Ourselves: ** (AA 67.3) * (AA 62.2)	Putting out of our mind the wrong others had done, we resolutely looked for our own mistakes... We admitted our wrongs honestly...** **STEPS 4** and/or **10 - (Column 4)**	
Where had I been selfish, self-centred or self-seeking?**		
Where had I been dishonest?**		
Where had I been frightened?**		
For what had I been responsible?**		
What decisions did I make based on self that later placed me in a position to be hurt?*		
When in the past did I make this decision? * (Earliest memory)		
Where was I wrong,** what was my part?		
STEPS 6 & 7 – List of Character Defects		
STEP 9 - Amends		**STEP 8**
		☐ Now ☐ Later ☐ Never

FOUR COLUMN INVENTORY...

COLUMN WORK

Resentment (1) and/or Fear:	The Cause (Column 2)	Affects Our: (Column 3)
Person, Place or Thing		☐ Self-Esteem ☐ Security ☐ Ambitions ☐ Personal Relations ☐ Sex Relations ☐ Pride/Shame ☐ Fear
Ask Ourselves: ** (AA 67.3) * (AA 62.2)	Putting out of our mind the wrong others had done, we resolutely looked for our own mistakes... We admitted our wrongs honestly...** **STEPS 4** and/or **10** - **(Column 4)**	
Where had I been selfish, self-centred or self-seeking?**		
Where had I been dishonest?**		
Where had I been frightened?**		
For what had I been responsible?**		
What decisions did I make based on self that later placed me in a position to be hurt?*		
When in the past did I make this decision? * (Earliest memory)		
Where was I wrong,** what was my part?		

STEPS 6 & 7 – List of Character Defects				

STEP 9 - Amends	STEP 8
	☐ Now ☐ Later ☐ Never

FORMS ONLY

INVENTORY FORMS

Resentment (1) and/or Fear:	The Cause (Column 2)	Affects Our: (Column 3)
Person, Place or Thing		☐ Self-Esteem ☐ Security ☐ Ambitions ☐ Personal Relations ☐ Sex Relations ☐ Pride/Shame ☐ Fear
Ask Ourselves: ** (AA 67.3) * (AA 62.2)	Putting out of our mind the wrong others had done, we resolutely looked for our own mistakes... We admitted our wrongs honestly...** **STEPS 4** and/or **10** - **(Column 4)**	
Where had I been selfish, self-centred or self-seeking?**		
Where had I been dishonest?**		
Where had I been frightened?**		
For what had I been responsible?**		
What decisions did I make based on self that later placed me in a position to be hurt?*		
When in the past did I make this decision? * (Earliest memory)		
Where was I wrong,** what was my part?		

STEPS 6 & 7 – List of Character Defects			

STEP 9 - Amends	STEP 8
	☐ Now ☐ Later ☐ Never

FOUR COLUMN INVENTORY...

COLUMN WORK

Resentment (1) and/or Fear:	The Cause (Column 2)	Affects Our: (Column 3)
Person, Place or Thing		☐ Self-Esteem ☐ Security ☐ Ambitions ☐ Personal Relations ☐ Sex Relations ☐ Pride/Shame ☐ Fear
Ask Ourselves: ** (AA 67.3) * (AA 62.2)	Putting out of our mind the wrong others had done, we resolutely looked for our own mistakes… We admitted our wrongs honestly…** STEPS 4 and/or 10 - (Column 4)	
Where had I been selfish, self-centred or self-seeking?**		
Where had I been dishonest?**		
Where had I been frightened?**		
For what had I been responsible?**		
What decisions did I make based on self that later placed me in a position to be hurt?*		
When in the past did I make this decision? * (Earliest memory)		
Where was I wrong,** what was my part?		
STEPS 6 & 7 – List of Character Defects		
---	---	---	---	---

STEP 9 - Amends	STEP 8
	☐ Now ☐ Later ☐ Never

FORMS ONLY

INVENTORY FORMS

Resentment (1) and/or Fear:	The Cause (Column 2)	Affects Our: (Column 3)
Person, Place or Thing		☐ Self-Esteem ☐ Security ☐ Ambitions ☐ Personal Relations ☐ Sex Relations ☐ Pride/Shame ☐ Fear
Ask Ourselves: ** (AA 67.3) * (AA 62.2)	Putting out of our mind the wrong others had done, we resolutely looked for our own mistakes... We admitted our wrongs honestly...** **STEPS 4** and/or **10** - **(Column 4)**	
Where had I been selfish, self-centred or self-seeking?**		
Where had I been dishonest?**		
Where had I been frightened?**		
For what had I been responsible?**		
What decisions did I make based on self that later placed me in a position to be hurt?*		
When in the past did I make this decision? * (Earliest memory)		
Where was I wrong,** what was my part?		

STEPS 6 & 7 – List of Character Defects			

STEP 9 - Amends	STEP 8
	☐ Now ☐ Later ☐ Never

FOUR COLUMN INVENTORY...

COLUMN WORK

Resentment (1) and/or Fear:	The Cause (Column 2)	Affects Our: (Column 3)
Person, Place or Thing		☐ Self-Esteem ☐ Security ☐ Ambitions ☐ Personal Relations ☐ Sex Relations ☐ Pride/Shame ☐ Fear
Ask Ourselves: ** (AA 67.3) * (AA 62.2)	Putting out of our mind the wrong others had done, we resolutely looked for our own mistakes... We admitted our wrongs honestly...** **STEPS 4 and/or 10 - (Column 4)**	
Where had I been selfish, self-centred or self-seeking?**		
Where had I been dishonest?**		
Where had I been frightened?**		
For what had I been responsible?**		
What decisions did I make based on self that later placed me in a position to be hurt?*		
When in the past did I make this decision? * (Earliest memory)		
Where was I wrong,** what was my part?		
STEPS 6 & 7 – List of Character Defects		
STEP 9 - Amends		**STEP 8**
		☐ Now ☐ Later ☐ Never

FORMS ONLY

INVENTORY FORMS

Resentment (1) and/or Fear:	The Cause (Column 2)	Affects Our: (Column 3)
Person, Place or Thing		☐ Self-Esteem ☐ Security ☐ Ambitions ☐ Personal Relations ☐ Sex Relations ☐ Pride/Shame ☐ Fear
Ask Ourselves: ** (AA 67.3) * (AA 62.2)	Putting out of our mind the wrong others had done, we resolutely looked for our own mistakes… We admitted our wrongs honestly…** **STEPS 4** and/or **10 - (Column 4)**	
Where had I been selfish, self-centred or self-seeking?**		
Where had I been dishonest?**		
Where had I been frightened?**		
For what had I been responsible?**		
What decisions did I make based on self that later placed me in a position to be hurt?*		
When in the past did I make this decision? * (Earliest memory)		
Where was I wrong,** what was my part?		
STEPS 6 & 7 – List of Character Defects		
STEP 9 - Amends		**STEP 8**
		☐ Now ☐ Later ☐ Never

FOUR COLUMN INVENTORY…

COLUMN WORK

Resentment (1) and/or Fear:	The Cause (Column 2)	Affects Our: (Column 3)
Person, Place or Thing		☐ Self-Esteem ☐ Security ☐ Ambitions ☐ Personal Relations ☐ Sex Relations ☐ Pride/Shame ☐ Fear
Ask Ourselves: ** (AA 67.3) * (AA 62.2)	Putting out of our mind the wrong others had done, we resolutely looked for our own mistakes… We admitted our wrongs honestly…** **STEPS 4** and/or **10** - **(Column 4)**	
Where had I been selfish, self-centred or self-seeking?**		
Where had I been dishonest?**		
Where had I been frightened?**		
For what had I been responsible?**		
What decisions did I make based on self that later placed me in a position to be hurt?*		
When in the past did I make this decision? * (Earliest memory)		
Where was I wrong,** what was my part?		

STEPS 6 & 7 – List of Character Defects			

STEP 9 - Amends	STEP 8
	☐ Now ☐ Later ☐ Never

FORMS ONLY

INVENTORY FORMS

Resentment (1) and/or Fear:	The Cause (Column 2)	Affects Our: (Column 3)
Person, Place or Thing		☐ Self-Esteem ☐ Security ☐ Ambitions ☐ Personal Relations ☐ Sex Relations ☐ Pride/Shame ☐ Fear
Ask Ourselves: ** (AA 67.3) * (AA 62.2)	Putting out of our mind the wrong others had done, we resolutely looked for our own mistakes... We admitted our wrongs honestly...** **STEPS 4 and/or 10 - (Column 4)**	
Where had I been selfish, self-centred or self-seeking?**		
Where had I been dishonest?**		
Where had I been frightened?**		
For what had I been responsible?**		
What decisions did I make based on self that later placed me in a position to be hurt?*		
When in the past did I make this decision? * (Earliest memory)		
Where was I wrong,** what was my part?		

STEPS 6 & 7 – List of Character Defects			

STEP 9 - Amends	STEP 8
	☐ Now ☐ Later ☐ Never

FOUR COLUMN INVENTORY...

COLUMN WORK

Resentment (1) and/or Fear:	The Cause (Column 2)	Affects Our: (Column 3)
Person, Place or Thing		☐ Self-Esteem ☐ Security ☐ Ambitions ☐ Personal Relations ☐ Sex Relations ☐ Pride/Shame ☐ Fear
Ask Ourselves: ** (AA 67.3) * (AA 62.2)	Putting out of our mind the wrong others had done, we resolutely looked for our own mistakes… We admitted our wrongs honestly…** **STEPS 4** and/or **10 - (Column 4)**	
Where had I been selfish, self-centred or self-seeking?**		
Where had I been dishonest?**		
Where had I been frightened?**		
For what had I been responsible?**		
What decisions did I make based on self that later placed me in a position to be hurt?*		
When in the past did I make this decision? * (Earliest memory)		
Where was I wrong,** what was my part?		

STEPS 6 & 7 – List of Character Defects			

STEP 9 - Amends	STEP 8
	☐ Now ☐ Later ☐ Never

FORMS ONLY

INVENTORY FORMS

Resentment (1) and/or Fear:	The Cause (Column 2)	Affects Our: (Column 3)
Person, Place or Thing		☐ Self-Esteem ☐ Security ☐ Ambitions ☐ Personal Relations ☐ Sex Relations ☐ Pride/Shame ☐ Fear
Ask Ourselves: ** (AA 67.3) * (AA 62.2)	Putting out of our mind the wrong others had done, we resolutely looked for our own mistakes... We admitted our wrongs honestly...** **STEPS 4** and/or **10** - **(Column 4)**	
Where had I been selfish, self-centred or self-seeking?**		
Where had I been dishonest?**		
Where had I been frightened?**		
For what had I been responsible?**		
What decisions did I make based on self that later placed me in a position to be hurt?*		
When in the past did I make this decision? * (Earliest memory)		
Where was I wrong,** what was my part?		
STEPS 6 & 7 – List of Character Defects		

STEP 9 - Amends	STEP 8
	☐ Now ☐ Later ☐ Never

FOUR COLUMN INVENTORY...

COLUMN WORK

Resentment (1) and/or Fear:	The Cause (Column 2)	Affects Our: (Column 3)
Person, Place or Thing		☐ Self-Esteem ☐ Security ☐ Ambitions ☐ Personal Relations ☐ Sex Relations ☐ Pride/Shame ☐ Fear
Ask Ourselves: ** (AA 67.3) * (AA 62.2)	Putting out of our mind the wrong others had done, we resolutely looked for our own mistakes… We admitted our wrongs honestly…** **STEPS 4** and/or **10** - **(Column 4)**	
Where had I been selfish, self-centred or self-seeking?**		
Where had I been dishonest?**		
Where had I been frightened?**		
For what had I been responsible?**		
What decisions did I make based on self that later placed me in a position to be hurt?*		
When in the past did I make this decision? * (Earliest memory)		
Where was I wrong,** what was my part?		

STEPS 6 & 7 – List of Character Defects

STEP 9 - Amends	STEP 8
	☐ Now ☐ Later ☐ Never

FORMS ONLY

INVENTORY FORMS

Resentment (1) and/or Fear:	The Cause (Column 2)	Affects Our: (Column 3)
Person, Place or Thing		☐ Self-Esteem ☐ Security ☐ Ambitions ☐ Personal Relations ☐ Sex Relations ☐ Pride/Shame ☐ Fear
Ask Ourselves: ** (AA 67.3) * (AA 62.2)	Putting out of our mind the wrong others had done, we resolutely looked for our own mistakes... We admitted our wrongs honestly...** **STEPS 4** and/or **10 - (Column 4)**	
Where had I been selfish, self-centred or self-seeking?**		
Where had I been dishonest?**		
Where had I been frightened?**		
For what had I been responsible?**		
What decisions did I make based on self that later placed me in a position to be hurt?*		
When in the past did I make this decision? * (Earliest memory)		
Where was I wrong,** what was my part?		

STEPS 6 & 7 – List of Character Defects

STEP 9 - Amends	STEP 8
	☐ Now ☐ Later ☐ Never

FOUR COLUMN INVENTORY...

COLUMN WORK

Resentment (1) and/or Fear:	The Cause (Column 2)	Affects Our: (Column 3)
Person, Place or Thing		☐ Self-Esteem ☐ Security ☐ Ambitions ☐ Personal Relations ☐ Sex Relations ☐ Pride/Shame ☐ Fear
Ask Ourselves: ** (AA 67.3) * (AA 62.2)	Putting out of our mind the wrong others had done, we resolutely looked for our own mistakes… We admitted our wrongs honestly…** **STEPS 4** and/or **10** - **(Column 4)**	
Where had I been selfish, self-centred or self-seeking?**		
Where had I been dishonest?**		
Where had I been frightened?**		
For what had I been responsible?**		
What decisions did I make based on self that later placed me in a position to be hurt?*		
When in the past did I make this decision? * (Earliest memory)		
Where was I wrong,** what was my part?		

STEPS 6 & 7 – List of Character Defects			

STEP 9 - Amends	STEP 8
	☐ Now ☐ Later ☐ Never

FORMS ONLY

INVENTORY FORMS

Resentment (1) and/or Fear:	The Cause (Column 2)	Affects Our: (Column 3)
Person, Place or Thing		☐ Self-Esteem ☐ Security ☐ Ambitions ☐ Personal Relations ☐ Sex Relations ☐ Pride/Shame ☐ Fear
Ask Ourselves: ** (AA 67.3) * (AA 62.2)	Putting out of our mind the wrong others had done, we resolutely looked for our own mistakes… We admitted our wrongs honestly…** **STEPS 4 and/or 10 - (Column 4)**	
Where had I been selfish, self-centred or self-seeking?**		
Where had I been dishonest?**		
Where had I been frightened?**		
For what had I been responsible?**		
What decisions did I make based on self that later placed me in a position to be hurt?*		
When in the past did I make this decision? * (Earliest memory)		
Where was I wrong,** what was my part?		

STEPS 6 & 7 – List of Character Defects			

STEP 9 - Amends	STEP 8
	☐ Now ☐ Later ☐ Never

FOUR COLUMN INVENTORY…

COLUMN WORK

Resentment (1) and/or Fear:	The Cause (Column 2)	Affects Our: (Column 3)
Person, Place or Thing		☐ Self-Esteem ☐ Security ☐ Ambitions ☐ Personal Relations ☐ Sex Relations ☐ Pride/Shame ☐ Fear
Ask Ourselves: ** (AA 67.3) * (AA 62.2)	Putting out of our mind the wrong others had done, we resolutely looked for our own mistakes... We admitted our wrongs honestly...** **STEPS 4 and/or 10 - (Column 4)**	
Where had I been selfish, self-centred or self-seeking?**		
Where had I been dishonest?**		
Where had I been frightened?**		
For what had I been responsible?**		
What decisions did I make based on self that later placed me in a position to be hurt?*		
When in the past did I make this decision? * (Earliest memory)		
Where was I wrong,** what was my part?		
STEPS 6 & 7 – List of Character Defects					

STEP 9 - Amends	STEP 8
	☐ Now ☐ Later ☐ Never

FORMS ONLY

INVENTORY FORMS

Resentment (1) and/or Fear:	The Cause (Column 2)	Affects Our: (Column 3)
Person, Place or Thing		☐ Self-Esteem ☐ Security ☐ Ambitions ☐ Personal Relations ☐ Sex Relations ☐ Pride/Shame ☐ Fear
Ask Ourselves: ** (AA 67.3) * (AA 62.2)	Putting out of our mind the wrong others had done, we resolutely looked for our own mistakes… We admitted our wrongs honestly…** **STEPS 4 and/or 10 - (Column 4)**	
Where had I been selfish, self-centred or self-seeking?**		
Where had I been dishonest?**		
Where had I been frightened?**		
For what had I been responsible?**		
What decisions did I make based on self that later placed me in a position to be hurt?*		
When in the past did I make this decision? * (Earliest memory)		
Where was I wrong,** what was my part?		

STEPS 6 & 7 – List of Character Defects			

STEP 9 - Amends	STEP 8
	☐ Now ☐ Later ☐ Never

FOUR COLUMN INVENTORY…

COLUMN WORK

Resentment (1) and/or Fear:	The Cause (Column 2)	Affects Our: (Column 3)
Person, Place or Thing		☐ Self-Esteem ☐ Security ☐ Ambitions ☐ Personal Relations ☐ Sex Relations ☐ Pride/Shame ☐ Fear
Ask Ourselves: ** (AA 67.3) * (AA 62.2)	Putting out of our mind the wrong others had done, we resolutely looked for our own mistakes... We admitted our wrongs honestly... ** **STEPS 4 and/or 10 - (Column 4)**	
Where had I been selfish, self-centred or self-seeking?**		
Where had I been dishonest?**		
Where had I been frightened?**		
For what had I been responsible?**		
What decisions did I make based on self that later placed me in a position to be hurt?*		
When in the past did I make this decision? * (Earliest memory)		
Where was I wrong,** what was my part?		

STEPS 6 & 7 – List of Character Defects

STEP 9 - Amends		STEP 8
		☐ Now ☐ Later ☐ Never

FORMS ONLY

INVENTORY FORMS

Resentment (1) and/or Fear:	The Cause (Column 2)	Affects Our: (Column 3)
Person, Place or Thing		☐ Self-Esteem ☐ Security ☐ Ambitions ☐ Personal Relations ☐ Sex Relations ☐ Pride/Shame ☐ Fear
Ask Ourselves: ** (AA 67.3) * (AA 62.2)	Putting out of our mind the wrong others had done, we resolutely looked for our own mistakes... We admitted our wrongs honestly...** **STEPS 4** and/or **10 - (Column 4)**	
Where had I been selfish, self-centred or self-seeking?**		
Where had I been dishonest?**		
Where had I been frightened?**		
For what had I been responsible?**		
What decisions did I make based on self that later placed me in a position to be hurt?*		
When in the past did I make this decision? * (Earliest memory)		
Where was I wrong,** what was my part?		

STEPS 6 & 7 – List of Character Defects			

STEP 9 - Amends	STEP 8
	☐ Now ☐ Later ☐ Never

FOUR COLUMN INVENTORY...

COLUMN WORK

Resentment (1) and/or Fear:	The Cause (Column 2)	Affects Our: (Column 3)
Person, Place or Thing		☐ Self-Esteem ☐ Security ☐ Ambitions ☐ Personal Relations ☐ Sex Relations ☐ Pride/Shame ☐ Fear
Ask Ourselves: ** (AA 67.3) * (AA 62.2)	Putting out of our mind the wrong others had done, we resolutely looked for our own mistakes… We admitted our wrongs honestly…** **STEPS 4 and/or 10 - (Column 4)**	
Where had I been selfish, self-centred or self-seeking?**		
Where had I been dishonest?**		
Where had I been frightened?**		
For what had I been responsible?**		
What decisions did I make based on self that later placed me in a position to be hurt?*		
When in the past did I make this decision? * (Earliest memory)		
Where was I wrong,** what was my part?		

STEPS 6 & 7 – List of Character Defects				

STEP 9 - Amends	STEP 8
	☐ Now ☐ Later ☐ Never

FORMS ONLY

INVENTORY FORMS

Resentment (1) and/or Fear:	The Cause (Column 2)	Affects Our: (Column 3)
Person, Place or Thing		☐ Self-Esteem ☐ Security ☐ Ambitions ☐ Personal Relations ☐ Sex Relations ☐ Pride/Shame ☐ Fear
Ask Ourselves: ** (AA 67.3) * (AA 62.2)	Putting out of our mind the wrong others had done, we resolutely looked for our own mistakes... We admitted our wrongs honestly...** **STEPS 4** and/or **10** - **(Column 4)**	
Where had I been selfish, self-centred or self-seeking?**		
Where had I been dishonest?**		
Where had I been frightened?**		
For what had I been responsible?**		
What decisions did I make based on self that later placed me in a position to be hurt?*		
When in the past did I make this decision? * (Earliest memory)		
Where was I wrong,** what was my part?		

STEPS 6 & 7 – List of Character Defects

STEP 9 - Amends	STEP 8
	☐ Now ☐ Later ☐ Never

COLUMN WORK

Resentment (1) and/or Fear:	The Cause (Column 2)	Affects Our: (Column 3)
Person, Place or Thing		☐ Self-Esteem ☐ Security ☐ Ambitions ☐ Personal Relations ☐ Sex Relations ☐ Pride/Shame ☐ Fear
Ask Ourselves: ** (AA 67.3) * (AA 62.2)	Putting out of our mind the wrong others had done, we resolutely looked for our own mistakes… We admitted our wrongs honestly…** **STEPS 4 and/or 10 - (Column 4)**	
Where had I been selfish, self-centred or self-seeking?**		
Where had I been dishonest?**		
Where had I been frightened?**		
For what had I been responsible?**		
What decisions did I make based on self that later placed me in a position to be hurt?*		
When in the past did I make this decision? * (Earliest memory)		
Where was I wrong,** what was my part?		
STEPS 6 & 7 – List of Character Defects		
STEP 9 - Amends		**STEP 8** ☐ Now ☐ Later ☐ Never

FORMS ONLY

INVENTORY FORMS

Resentment (1) and/or Fear:	The Cause (Column 2)	Affects Our: (Column 3)
Person, Place or Thing		☐ Self-Esteem ☐ Security ☐ Ambitions ☐ Personal Relations ☐ Sex Relations ☐ Pride/Shame ☐ Fear
Ask Ourselves: ** (AA 67.3) * (AA 62.2)	Putting out of our mind the wrong others had done, we resolutely looked for our own mistakes... We admitted our wrongs honestly...** **STEPS 4** and/or **10** - **(Column 4)**	
Where had I been selfish, self-centred or self-seeking?**		
Where had I been dishonest?**		
Where had I been frightened?**		
For what had I been responsible?**		
What decisions did I make based on self that later placed me in a position to be hurt?*		
When in the past did I make this decision? * (Earliest memory)		
Where was I wrong,** what was my part?		
STEPS 6 & 7 – List of Character Defects		
STEP 9 - Amends		**STEP 8**
		☐ Now ☐ Later ☐ Never

FOUR COLUMN INVENTORY...

COLUMN WORK

Resentment and/or Fear: (1)	The Cause (Column 2)	Affects Our: (Column 3)
Person, Place or Thing		☐ Self-Esteem ☐ Security ☐ Ambitions ☐ Personal Relations ☐ Sex Relations ☐ Pride/Shame ☐ Fear
Ask Ourselves: ** (AA 67.3) * (AA 62.2)	Putting out of our mind the wrong others had done, we resolutely looked for our own mistakes… We admitted our wrongs honestly…** **STEPS 4** and/or **10** - **(Column 4)**	
Where had I been selfish, self-centred or self-seeking?**		
Where had I been dishonest?**		
Where had I been frightened?**		
For what had I been responsible?**		
What decisions did I make based on self that later placed me in a position to be hurt?*		
When in the past did I make this decision? * (Earliest memory)		
Where was I wrong,** what was my part?		

STEPS 6 & 7 – List of Character Defects

STEP 9 - Amends	STEP 8
	☐ Now ☐ Later ☐ Never

INVENTORY FORMS

Resentment (1) and/or Fear:	The Cause (Column 2)	Affects Our: (Column 3)
Person, Place or Thing		☐ Self-Esteem ☐ Security ☐ Ambitions ☐ Personal Relations ☐ Sex Relations ☐ Pride/Shame ☐ Fear
Ask Ourselves: ** (AA 67.3) * (AA 62.2)	Putting out of our mind the wrong others had done, we resolutely looked for our own mistakes... We admitted our wrongs honestly...** **STEPS 4** and/or **10 - (Column 4)**	
Where had I been selfish, self-centred or self-seeking?**		
Where had I been dishonest?**		
Where had I been frightened?**		
For what had I been responsible?**		
What decisions did I make based on self that later placed me in a position to be hurt?*		
When in the past did I make this decision? * (Earliest memory)		
Where was I wrong,** what was my part?		
STEPS 6 & 7 – List of Character Defects			
STEP 9 - Amends		**STEP 8**
		☐ Now ☐ Later ☐ Never

COLUMN WORK

Resentment (1) and/or Fear:	The Cause (Column 2)	Affects Our: (Column 3)
Person, Place or Thing		☐ Self-Esteem ☐ Security ☐ Ambitions ☐ Personal Relations ☐ Sex Relations ☐ Pride/Shame ☐ Fear
Ask Ourselves: ** (AA 67.3) * (AA 62.2)	Putting out of our mind the wrong others had done, we resolutely looked for our own mistakes… We admitted our wrongs honestly…** **STEPS 4** and/or **10 - (Column 4)**	
Where had I been selfish, self-centred or self-seeking?**		
Where had I been dishonest?**		
Where had I been frightened?**		
For what had I been responsible?**		
What decisions did I make based on self that later placed me in a position to be hurt?*		
When in the past did I make this decision? * (Earliest memory)		
Where was I wrong,** what was my part?		

STEPS 6 & 7 – List of Character Defects

STEP 9 - Amends	STEP 8
	☐ Now ☐ Later ☐ Never

FORMS ONLY

INVENTORY FORMS

Resentment (1) and/or Fear:	The Cause (Column 2)	Affects Our: (Column 3)
Person, Place or Thing		☐ Self-Esteem ☐ Security ☐ Ambitions ☐ Personal Relations ☐ Sex Relations ☐ Pride/Shame ☐ Fear
Ask Ourselves: ** (AA 67.3) * (AA 62.2)	Putting out of our mind the wrong others had done, we resolutely looked for our own mistakes... We admitted our wrongs honestly...** **STEPS 4** and/or **10** - **(Column 4)**	
Where had I been selfish, self-centred or self-seeking?**		
Where had I been dishonest?**		
Where had I been frightened?**		
For what had I been responsible?**		
What decisions did I make based on self that later placed me in a position to be hurt?*		
When in the past did I make this decision? * (Earliest memory)		
Where was I wrong,** what was my part?		
STEPS 6 & 7 – List of Character Defects			
STEP 9 - Amends			**STEP 8**
			☐ **Now** ☐ **Later** ☐ **Never**

FOUR COLUMN INVENTORY...

COLUMN WORK

Resentment (1) and/or Fear:	The Cause (Column 2)	Affects Our: (Column 3)
Person, Place or Thing		☐ Self-Esteem ☐ Security ☐ Ambitions ☐ Personal Relations ☐ Sex Relations ☐ Pride/Shame ☐ Fear
Ask Ourselves: ** (AA 67.3) * (AA 62.2)	Putting out of our mind the wrong others had done, we resolutely looked for our own mistakes… We admitted our wrongs honestly…** **STEPS 4** and/or **10** - **(Column 4)**	
Where had I been selfish, self-centred or self-seeking?**		
Where had I been dishonest?**		
Where had I been frightened?**		
For what had I been responsible?**		
What decisions did I make based on self that later placed me in a position to be hurt?*		
When in the past did I make this decision? * (Earliest memory)		
Where was I wrong,** what was my part?		

STEPS 6 & 7 – List of Character Defects			

STEP 9 - Amends	STEP 8
	☐ Now ☐ Later ☐ Never

FORMS ONLY

INVENTORY FORMS

Resentment (1) and/or Fear:	The Cause (Column 2)	Affects Our: (Column 3)
Person, Place or Thing		☐ Self-Esteem ☐ Security ☐ Ambitions ☐ Personal Relations ☐ Sex Relations ☐ Pride/Shame ☐ Fear
Ask Ourselves: ** (AA 67.3) * (AA 62.2)	Putting out of our mind the wrong others had done, we resolutely looked for our own mistakes... We admitted our wrongs honestly...** **STEPS 4** and/or **10 - (Column 4)**	
Where had I been selfish, self-centred or self-seeking?**		
Where had I been dishonest?**		
Where had I been frightened?**		
For what had I been responsible?**		
What decisions did I make based on self that later placed me in a position to be hurt?*		
When in the past did I make this decision? * (Earliest memory)		
Where was I wrong,** what was my part?		

STEPS 6 & 7 – List of Character Defects			

STEP 9 - Amends	STEP 8
	☐ Now ☐ Later ☐ Never

FOUR COLUMN INVENTORY...

COLUMN WORK

Resentment (1) and/or Fear:	The Cause (Column 2)	Affects Our: (Column 3)
Person, Place or Thing		☐ Self-Esteem ☐ Security ☐ Ambitions ☐ Personal Relations ☐ Sex Relations ☐ Pride/Shame ☐ Fear
Ask Ourselves: ** (AA 67.3) * (AA 62.2)	Putting out of our mind the wrong others had done, we resolutely looked for our own mistakes… We admitted our wrongs honestly…** **STEPS 4** and/or **10** - **(Column 4)**	
Where had I been selfish, self-centred or self-seeking?**		
Where had I been dishonest?**		
Where had I been frightened?**		
For what had I been responsible?**		
What decisions did I make based on self that later placed me in a position to be hurt?*		
When in the past did I make this decision? * (Earliest memory)		
Where was I wrong,** what was my part?		

STEPS 6 & 7 – List of Character Defects			

STEP 9 - Amends	STEP 8
	☐ Now ☐ Later ☐ Never

INVENTORY FORMS

Resentment (1) and/or Fear:	The Cause (Column 2)	Affects Our: (Column 3)
Person, Place or Thing		☐ Self-Esteem ☐ Security ☐ Ambitions ☐ Personal Relations ☐ Sex Relations ☐ Pride/Shame ☐ Fear
Ask Ourselves: ** (AA 67.3) * (AA 62.2)	Putting out of our mind the wrong others had done, we resolutely looked for our own mistakes… We admitted our wrongs honestly…** **STEPS 4** and/or **10** - **(Column 4)**	
Where had I been selfish, self-centred or self-seeking?**		
Where had I been dishonest?**		
Where had I been frightened?**		
For what had I been responsible?**		
What decisions did I make based on self that later placed me in a position to be hurt?*		
When in the past did I make this decision? * (Earliest memory)		
Where was I wrong,** what was my part?		
STEPS 6 & 7 – List of Character Defects		
STEP 9 - Amends		**STEP 8**
		☐ Now ☐ Later ☐ Never

58   FOUR COLUMN INVENTORY…

COLUMN WORK

Resentment (1) and/or Fear:	The Cause (Column 2)	Affects Our: (Column 3)
Person, Place or Thing		☐ Self-Esteem ☐ Security ☐ Ambitions ☐ Personal Relations ☐ Sex Relations ☐ Pride/Shame ☐ Fear
Ask Ourselves: ** (AA 67.3) * (AA 62.2)	Putting out of our mind the wrong others had done, we resolutely looked for our own mistakes… We admitted our wrongs honestly…** **STEPS 4** and/or **10 - (Column 4)**	
Where had I been selfish, self-centred or self-seeking?**		
Where had I been dishonest?**		
Where had I been frightened?**		
For what had I been responsible?**		
What decisions did I make based on self that later placed me in a position to be hurt?*		
When in the past did I make this decision? * (Earliest memory)		
Where was I wrong,** what was my part?		

STEPS 6 & 7 – List of Character Defects

STEP 9 - Amends | STEP 8

	☐ Now ☐ Later ☐ Never

FORMS ONLY

INVENTORY FORMS

Resentment (1) and/or Fear:	The Cause (Column 2)	Affects Our: (Column 3)
Person, Place or Thing		☐ Self-Esteem ☐ Security ☐ Ambitions ☐ Personal Relations ☐ Sex Relations ☐ Pride/Shame ☐ Fear
Ask Ourselves: ** (AA 67.3) * (AA 62.2)	Putting out of our mind the wrong others had done, we resolutely looked for our own mistakes… We admitted our wrongs honestly…** **STEPS 4 and/or 10 - (Column 4)**	
Where had I been selfish, self-centred or self-seeking?**		
Where had I been dishonest?**		
Where had I been frightened?**		
For what had I been responsible?**		
What decisions did I make based on self that later placed me in a position to be hurt?*		
When in the past did I make this decision? * (Earliest memory)		
Where was I wrong,** what was my part?		

STEPS 6 & 7 – List of Character Defects			

STEP 9 - Amends			STEP 8
			☐ Now ☐ Later ☐ Never

FOUR COLUMN INVENTORY…

COLUMN WORK

Resentment and/or Fear: (1)	The Cause (Column 2)	Affects Our: (Column 3)
Person, Place or Thing		☐ Self-Esteem ☐ Security ☐ Ambitions ☐ Personal Relations ☐ Sex Relations ☐ Pride/Shame ☐ Fear
Ask Ourselves: ** (AA 67.3) * (AA 62.2)	Putting out of our mind the wrong others had done, we resolutely looked for our own mistakes... We admitted our wrongs honestly...** **STEPS 4** and/or **10** - (Column 4)	
Where had I been selfish, self-centred or self-seeking?**		
Where had I been dishonest?**		
Where had I been frightened?**		
For what had I been responsible?**		
What decisions did I make based on self that later placed me in a position to be hurt?*		
When in the past did I make this decision? * (Earliest memory)		
Where was I wrong,** what was my part?		

STEPS 6 & 7 – List of Character Defects			

STEP 9 - Amends	STEP 8
	☐ Now ☐ Later ☐ Never

FORMS ONLY

INVENTORY FORMS

Resentment (1) and/or Fear:	The Cause (Column 2)	Affects Our: (Column 3)
Person, Place or Thing		☐ Self-Esteem ☐ Security ☐ Ambitions ☐ Personal Relations ☐ Sex Relations ☐ Pride/Shame ☐ Fear
Ask Ourselves: ** (AA 67.3) * (AA 62.2)	Putting out of our mind the wrong others had done, we resolutely looked for our own mistakes... We admitted our wrongs honestly...** **STEPS 4** and/or **10** - **(Column 4)**	
Where had I been selfish, self-centred or self-seeking?**		
Where had I been dishonest?**		
Where had I been frightened?**		
For what had I been responsible?**		
What decisions did I make based on self that later placed me in a position to be hurt?*		
When in the past did I make this decision? * (Earliest memory)		
Where was I wrong,** what was my part?		

STEPS 6 & 7 – List of Character Defects			

STEP 9 - Amends	STEP 8
	☐ Now ☐ Later ☐ Never

FOUR COLUMN INVENTORY...

COLUMN WORK

Resentment (1) and/or Fear:	The Cause (Column 2)	Affects Our: (Column 3)
Person, Place or Thing		☐ Self-Esteem ☐ Security ☐ Ambitions ☐ Personal Relations ☐ Sex Relations ☐ Pride/Shame ☐ Fear
Ask Ourselves: ** (AA 67.3) * (AA 62.2)	Putting out of our mind the wrong others had done, we resolutely looked for our own mistakes… We admitted our wrongs honestly…** **STEPS 4** and/or **10** - **(Column 4)**	
Where had I been selfish, self-centred or self-seeking?**		
Where had I been dishonest?**		
Where had I been frightened?**		
For what had I been responsible?**		
What decisions did I make based on self that later placed me in a position to be hurt?*		
When in the past did I make this decision? * (Earliest memory)		
Where was I wrong,** what was my part?		

STEPS 6 & 7 – List of Character Defects				

STEP 9 - Amends	STEP 8
	☐ Now ☐ Later ☐ Never

FORMS ONLY

INVENTORY FORMS

Resentment (1) and/or Fear:	The Cause (Column 2)	Affects Our: (Column 3)
Person, Place or Thing		☐ Self-Esteem ☐ Security ☐ Ambitions ☐ Personal Relations ☐ Sex Relations ☐ Pride/Shame ☐ Fear
Ask Ourselves: ** (AA 67.3) * (AA 62.2)	Putting out of our mind the wrong others had done, we resolutely looked for our own mistakes… We admitted our wrongs honestly…** **STEPS 4** and/or **10** - **(Column 4)**	
Where had I been selfish, self-centred or self-seeking?**		
Where had I been dishonest?**		
Where had I been frightened?**		
For what had I been responsible?**		
What decisions did I make based on self that later placed me in a position to be hurt?*		
When in the past did I make this decision? * (Earliest memory)		
Where was I wrong,** what was my part?		

STEPS 6 & 7 – List of Character Defects			

STEP 9 - Amends	STEP 8
	☐ Now ☐ Later ☐ Never

FOUR COLUMN INVENTORY…

COLUMN WORK

Resentment (1) and/or Fear:	The Cause (Column 2)	Affects Our: (Column 3)
Person, Place or Thing		☐ Self-Esteem ☐ Security ☐ Ambitions ☐ Personal Relations ☐ Sex Relations ☐ Pride/Shame ☐ Fear
Ask Ourselves: ** (AA 67.3) * (AA 62.2)	Putting out of our mind the wrong others had done, we resolutely looked for our own mistakes... We admitted our wrongs honestly... ** **STEPS 4 and/or 10 - (Column 4)**	
Where had I been selfish, self-centred or self-seeking?**		
Where had I been dishonest?**		
Where had I been frightened?**		
For what had I been responsible?**		
What decisions did I make based on self that later placed me in a position to be hurt?*		
When in the past did I make this decision? * (Earliest memory)		
Where was I wrong,** what was my part?		

STEPS 6 & 7 – List of Character Defects				

STEP 9 - Amends	STEP 8
	☐ Now ☐ Later ☐ Never

INVENTORY FORMS

Resentment (1) and/or Fear:	The Cause (Column 2)	Affects Our: (Column 3)
Person, Place or Thing		☐ Self-Esteem ☐ Security ☐ Ambitions ☐ Personal Relations ☐ Sex Relations ☐ Pride/Shame ☐ Fear
Ask Ourselves: ** (AA 67.3) * (AA 62.2)	Putting out of our mind the wrong others had done, we resolutely looked for our own mistakes... We admitted our wrongs honestly...** **STEPS 4 and/or 10 - (Column 4)**	
Where had I been selfish, self-centred or self-seeking?**		
Where had I been dishonest?**		
Where had I been frightened?**		
For what had I been responsible?**		
What decisions did I make based on self that later placed me in a position to be hurt?*		
When in the past did I make this decision? * (Earliest memory)		
Where was I wrong,** what was my part?		
STEPS 6 & 7 – List of Character Defects		
STEP 9 - Amends		**STEP 8**
		☐ Now ☐ Later ☐ Never

FOUR COLUMN INVENTORY...

COLUMN WORK

Resentment (1) and/or Fear:	The Cause (Column 2)	Affects Our: (Column 3)
Person, Place or Thing		☐ Self-Esteem ☐ Security ☐ Ambitions ☐ Personal Relations ☐ Sex Relations ☐ Pride/Shame ☐ Fear
Ask Ourselves: ** (AA 67.3) * (AA 62.2)	Putting out of our mind the wrong others had done, we resolutely looked for our own mistakes... We admitted our wrongs honestly... ** **STEPS 4** and/or **10 - (Column 4)**	
Where had I been selfish, self-centred or self-seeking?**		
Where had I been dishonest?**		
Where had I been frightened?**		
For what had I been responsible?**		
What decisions did I make based on self that later placed me in a position to be hurt?*		
When in the past did I make this decision? * (Earliest memory)		
Where was I wrong,** what was my part?		
STEPS 6 & 7 – List of Character Defects		
STEP 9 - Amends		**STEP 8**
		☐ Now ☐ Later ☐ Never

FORMS ONLY

INVENTORY FORMS

Resentment (1) and/or Fear:	The Cause (Column 2)	Affects Our: (Column 3)
Person, Place or Thing		☐ Self-Esteem ☐ Security ☐ Ambitions ☐ Personal Relations ☐ Sex Relations ☐ Pride/Shame ☐ Fear
Ask Ourselves: ** (AA 67.3) * (AA 62.2)	Putting out of our mind the wrong others had done, we resolutely looked for our own mistakes... We admitted our wrongs honestly... ** **STEPS 4** and/or **10** - **(Column 4)**	
Where had I been selfish, self-centred or self-seeking?**		
Where had I been dishonest?**		
Where had I been frightened?**		
For what had I been responsible?**		
What decisions did I make based on self that later placed me in a position to be hurt?*		
When in the past did I make this decision? * (Earliest memory)		
Where was I wrong,** what was my part?		

STEPS 6 & 7 – List of Character Defects			

STEP 9 - Amends	STEP 8
	☐ Now ☐ Later ☐ Never

FOUR COLUMN INVENTORY...

COLUMN WORK

Resentment (1) and/or Fear:	The Cause (Column 2)	Affects Our: (Column 3)
Person, Place or Thing		☐ Self-Esteem ☐ Security ☐ Ambitions ☐ Personal Relations ☐ Sex Relations ☐ Pride/Shame ☐ Fear
Ask Ourselves: ** (AA 67.3) * (AA 62.2)	Putting out of our mind the wrong others had done, we resolutely looked for our own mistakes… We admitted our wrongs honestly….** **STEPS 4** and/or **10** - **(Column 4)**	
Where had I been selfish, self-centred or self-seeking?**		
Where had I been dishonest?**		
Where had I been frightened?**		
For what had I been responsible?**		
What decisions did I make based on self that later placed me in a position to be hurt?*		
When in the past did I make this decision? * (Earliest memory)		
Where was I wrong,** what was my part?		

STEPS 6 & 7 – List of Character Defects

STEP 9 - Amends	STEP 8
	☐ Now ☐ Later ☐ Never

FORMS ONLY

INVENTORY FORMS

Resentment (1) and/or Fear:	The Cause (Column 2)	Affects Our: (Column 3)
Person, Place or Thing		☐ Self-Esteem ☐ Security ☐ Ambitions ☐ Personal Relations ☐ Sex Relations ☐ Pride/Shame ☐ Fear
Ask Ourselves: ** (AA 67.3) * (AA 62.2)	Putting out of our mind the wrong others had done, we resolutely looked for our own mistakes… We admitted our wrongs honestly…** **STEPS 4** and/or **10 - (Column 4)**	
Where had I been selfish, self-centred or self-seeking?**		
Where had I been dishonest?**		
Where had I been frightened?**		
For what had I been responsible?**		
What decisions did I make based on self that later placed me in a position to be hurt?*		
When in the past did I make this decision? * (Earliest memory)		
Where was I wrong,** what was my part?		

STEPS 6 & 7 – List of Character Defects			

STEP 9 - Amends	STEP 8
	☐ Now ☐ Later ☐ Never

COLUMN WORK

Resentment (1) and/or Fear:	The Cause (Column 2)	Affects Our: (Column 3)
Person, Place or Thing		☐ Self-Esteem ☐ Security ☐ Ambitions ☐ Personal Relations ☐ Sex Relations ☐ Pride/Shame ☐ Fear
Ask Ourselves: ** (AA 67.3) * (AA 62.2)	Putting out of our mind the wrong others had done, we resolutely looked for our own mistakes... We admitted our wrongs honestly...** **STEPS 4 and/or 10 - (Column 4)**	
Where had I been selfish, self-centred or self-seeking?**		
Where had I been dishonest?**		
Where had I been frightened?**		
For what had I been responsible?**		
What decisions did I make based on self that later placed me in a position to be hurt?*		
When in the past did I make this decision? * (Earliest memory)		
Where was I wrong,** what was my part?		

STEPS 6 & 7 – List of Character Defects				

STEP 9 - Amends	STEP 8
	☐ Now ☐ Later ☐ Never

FORMS ONLY

INVENTORY FORMS

Resentment (1) and/or Fear:	The Cause (Column 2)	Affects Our: (Column 3)
Person, Place or Thing		☐ Self-Esteem ☐ Security ☐ Ambitions ☐ Personal Relations ☐ Sex Relations ☐ Pride/Shame ☐ Fear
Ask Ourselves: ** (AA 67.3) * (AA 62.2)	Putting out of our mind the wrong others had done, we resolutely looked for our own mistakes... We admitted our wrongs honestly...** **STEPS 4** and/or **10 - (Column 4)**	
Where had I been selfish, self-centred or self-seeking?**		
Where had I been dishonest?**		
Where had I been frightened?**		
For what had I been responsible?**		
What decisions did I make based on self that later placed me in a position to be hurt?*		
When in the past did I make this decision? * (Earliest memory)		
Where was I wrong,** what was my part?		

STEPS 6 & 7 – List of Character Defects			

STEP 9 - Amends	STEP 8
	☐ Now ☐ Later ☐ Never

FOUR COLUMN INVENTORY...

COLUMN WORK

Resentment (1) and/or Fear:	The Cause (Column 2)	Affects Our: (Column 3)
Person, Place or Thing		☐ Self-Esteem ☐ Security ☐ Ambitions ☐ Personal Relations ☐ Sex Relations ☐ Pride/Shame ☐ Fear
Ask Ourselves: ** (AA 67.3) * (AA 62.2)	Putting out of our mind the wrong others had done, we resolutely looked for our own mistakes... We admitted our wrongs honestly...** **STEPS 4** and/or **10** - **(Column 4)**	
Where had I been selfish, self-centred or self-seeking?**		
Where had I been dishonest?**		
Where had I been frightened?**		
For what had I been responsible?**		
What decisions did I make based on self that later placed me in a position to be hurt?*		
When in the past did I make this decision? * (Earliest memory)		
Where was I wrong,** what was my part?		

STEPS 6 & 7 – List of Character Defects

STEP 9 - Amends	STEP 8
	☐ Now ☐ Later ☐ Never

FORMS ONLY

INVENTORY FORMS

Resentment (1) and/or Fear:	The Cause (Column 2)	Affects Our: (Column 3)
Person, Place or Thing		☐ Self-Esteem ☐ Security ☐ Ambitions ☐ Personal Relations ☐ Sex Relations ☐ Pride/Shame ☐ Fear
Ask Ourselves: ** (AA 67.3) * (AA 62.2)	Putting out of our mind the wrong others had done, we resolutely looked for our own mistakes... We admitted our wrongs honestly...** **STEPS 4** and/or **10** - **(Column 4)**	
Where had I been selfish, self-centred or self-seeking?**		
Where had I been dishonest?**		
Where had I been frightened?**		
For what had I been responsible?**		
What decisions did I make based on self that later placed me in a position to be hurt?*		
When in the past did I make this decision? * (Earliest memory)		
Where was I wrong,** what was my part?		

STEPS 6 & 7 – List of Character Defects			

STEP 9 - Amends	STEP 8
	☐ Now ☐ Later ☐ Never

COLUMN WORK

Resentment (1) and/or Fear:	The Cause (Column 2)	Affects Our: (Column 3)
Person, Place or Thing		☐ Self-Esteem ☐ Security ☐ Ambitions ☐ Personal Relations ☐ Sex Relations ☐ Pride/Shame ☐ Fear
Ask Ourselves: ** (AA 67.3) * (AA 62.2)	Putting out of our mind the wrong others had done, we resolutely looked for our own mistakes… We admitted our wrongs honestly…** **STEPS 4** and/or **10** - **(Column 4)**	
Where had I been selfish, self-centred or self-seeking?**		
Where had I been dishonest?**		
Where had I been frightened?**		
For what had I been responsible?**		
What decisions did I make based on self that later placed me in a position to be hurt?*		
When in the past did I make this decision? * (Earliest memory)		
Where was I wrong,** what was my part?		

STEPS 6 & 7 – List of Character Defects				

STEP 9 - Amends	STEP 8
	☐ Now ☐ Later ☐ Never

FORMS ONLY

INVENTORY FORMS

Resentment (1) and/or Fear:	The Cause (Column 2)	Affects Our: (Column 3)
Person, Place or Thing		☐ Self-Esteem ☐ Security ☐ Ambitions ☐ Personal Relations ☐ Sex Relations ☐ Pride/Shame ☐ Fear
Ask Ourselves: ** (AA 67.3) * (AA 62.2)	Putting out of our mind the wrong others had done, we resolutely looked for our own mistakes... We admitted our wrongs honestly...** **STEPS 4** and/or **10** - **(Column 4)**	
Where had I been selfish, self-centred or self-seeking?**		
Where had I been dishonest?**		
Where had I been frightened?**		
For what had I been responsible?**		
What decisions did I make based on self that later placed me in a position to be hurt?*		
When in the past did I make this decision? * (Earliest memory)		
Where was I wrong,** what was my part?		
STEPS 6 & 7 – List of Character Defects		
STEP 9 - Amends		**STEP 8**
		☐ Now ☐ Later ☐ Never

FOUR COLUMN INVENTORY...

COLUMN WORK

Resentment (1) and/or Fear:	The Cause (Column 2)	Affects Our: (Column 3)
Person, Place or Thing		☐ Self-Esteem ☐ Security ☐ Ambitions ☐ Personal Relations ☐ Sex Relations ☐ Pride/Shame ☐ Fear
Ask Ourselves: ** (AA 67.3) * (AA 62.2)	Putting out of our mind the wrong others had done, we resolutely looked for our own mistakes… We admitted our wrongs honestly…** **STEPS 4 and/or 10 - (Column 4)**	
Where had I been selfish, self-centred or self-seeking?**		
Where had I been dishonest?**		
Where had I been frightened?**		
For what had I been responsible?**		
What decisions did I make based on self that later placed me in a position to be hurt?*		
When in the past did I make this decision? * (Earliest memory)		
Where was I wrong,** what was my part?		

STEPS 6 & 7 – List of Character Defects				

STEP 9 - Amends	STEP 8
	☐ Now ☐ Later ☐ Never

FORMS ONLY

INVENTORY FORMS

Resentment (1) and/or Fear:	The Cause (Column 2)	Affects Our: (Column 3)
Person, Place or Thing		☐ Self-Esteem ☐ Security ☐ Ambitions ☐ Personal Relations ☐ Sex Relations ☐ Pride/Shame ☐ Fear
Ask Ourselves: ** (AA 67.3) * (AA 62.2)	Putting out of our mind the wrong others had done, we resolutely looked for our own mistakes... We admitted our wrongs honestly... ** **STEPS 4 and/or 10 - (Column 4)**	
Where had I been selfish, self-centred or self-seeking?**		
Where had I been dishonest?**		
Where had I been frightened?**		
For what had I been responsible?**		
What decisions did I make based on self that later placed me in a position to be hurt?*		
When in the past did I make this decision? * (Earliest memory)		
Where was I wrong,** what was my part?		

STEPS 6 & 7 – List of Character Defects			

STEP 9 - Amends	STEP 8
	☐ Now ☐ Later ☐ Never

FOUR COLUMN INVENTORY...

COLUMN WORK

Resentment (1) and/or Fear:	The Cause (Column 2)	Affects Our: (Column 3)
Person, Place or Thing		☐ Self-Esteem ☐ Security ☐ Ambitions ☐ Personal Relations ☐ Sex Relations ☐ Pride/Shame ☐ Fear
Ask Ourselves: ** (AA 67.3) * (AA 62.2)	Putting out of our mind the wrong others had done, we resolutely looked for our own mistakes… We admitted our wrongs honestly…** **STEPS 4** and/or **10** - **(Column 4)**	
Where had I been selfish, self-centred or self-seeking?**		
Where had I been dishonest?**		
Where had I been frightened?**		
For what had I been responsible?**		
What decisions did I make based on self that later placed me in a position to be hurt?*		
When in the past did I make this decision? * (Earliest memory)		
Where was I wrong,** what was my part?		

STEPS 6 & 7 – List of Character Defects

STEP 9 - Amends | STEP 8

☐ Now
☐ Later
☐ Never

FORMS ONLY

INVENTORY FORMS

Resentment (1) and/or Fear:	The Cause (Column 2)	Affects Our: (Column 3)
Person, Place or Thing		☐ Self-Esteem ☐ Security ☐ Ambitions ☐ Personal Relations ☐ Sex Relations ☐ Pride/Shame ☐ Fear
Ask Ourselves: ** (AA 67.3) * (AA 62.2)	Putting out of our mind the wrong others had done, we resolutely looked for our own mistakes... We admitted our wrongs honestly...** **STEPS 4** and/or **10 - (Column 4)**	
Where had I been selfish, self-centred or self-seeking?**		
Where had I been dishonest?**		
Where had I been frightened?**		
For what had I been responsible?**		
What decisions did I make based on self that later placed me in a position to be hurt?*		
When in the past did I make this decision? * (Earliest memory)		
Where was I wrong,** what was my part?		
STEPS 6 & 7 – List of Character Defects		
STEP 9 - Amends		**STEP 8**
		☐ Now ☐ Later ☐ Never

FOUR COLUMN INVENTORY...

COLUMN WORK

Resentment and/or Fear: (1)	The Cause (Column 2)	Affects Our: (Column 3)
Person, Place or Thing		☐ Self-Esteem ☐ Security ☐ Ambitions ☐ Personal Relations ☐ Sex Relations ☐ Pride/Shame ☐ Fear
Ask Ourselves: ** (AA 67.3) * (AA 62.2)	*Putting out of our mind the wrong others had done, we resolutely looked for our own mistakes... We admitted our wrongs honestly...*** **STEPS 4** and/or **10** - **(Column 4)**	
Where had I been selfish, self-centred or self-seeking?**		
Where had I been dishonest?**		
Where had I been frightened?**		
For what had I been responsible?**		
What decisions did I make based on self that later placed me in a position to be hurt?*		
When in the past did I make this decision? * (Earliest memory)		
Where was I wrong,** what was my part?		

STEPS 6 & 7 – List of Character Defects				

STEP 9 - Amends	STEP 8
	☐ Now ☐ Later ☐ Never

FORMS ONLY

INVENTORY FORMS

Resentment (1) and/or Fear:	The Cause (Column 2)	Affects Our: (Column 3)
Person, Place or Thing		☐ Self-Esteem ☐ Security ☐ Ambitions ☐ Personal Relations ☐ Sex Relations ☐ Pride/Shame ☐ Fear
Ask Ourselves: ** (AA 67.3) * (AA 62.2)	Putting out of our mind the wrong others had done, we resolutely looked for our own mistakes... We admitted our wrongs honestly...** **STEPS 4** and/or **10 - (Column 4)**	
Where had I been selfish, self-centred or self-seeking?**		
Where had I been dishonest?**		
Where had I been frightened?**		
For what had I been responsible?**		
What decisions did I make based on self that later placed me in a position to be hurt?*		
When in the past did I make this decision? * (Earliest memory)		
Where was I wrong,** what was my part?		
STEPS 6 & 7 – List of Character Defects		
STEP 9 - Amends		**STEP 8**
		☐ Now ☐ Later ☐ Never

FOUR COLUMN INVENTORY...

COLUMN WORK

Resentment (1) and/or Fear:	The Cause (Column 2)	Affects Our: (Column 3)
Person, Place or Thing		☐ Self-Esteem ☐ Security ☐ Ambitions ☐ Personal Relations ☐ Sex Relations ☐ Pride/Shame ☐ Fear
Ask Ourselves: ** (AA 67.3) * (AA 62.2)	Putting out of our mind the wrong others had done, we resolutely looked for our own mistakes… We admitted our wrongs honestly…** **STEPS 4** and/or **10 - (Column 4)**	
Where had I been selfish, self-centred or self-seeking?**		
Where had I been dishonest?**		
Where had I been frightened?**		
For what had I been responsible?**		
What decisions did I make based on self that later placed me in a position to be hurt?*		
When in the past did I make this decision? * (Earliest memory)		
Where was I wrong,** what was my part?		

STEPS 6 & 7 – List of Character Defects

STEP 9 - Amends	STEP 8
	☐ Now ☐ Later ☐ Never

FORMS ONLY

INVENTORY FORMS

Resentment (1) and/or Fear:	The Cause (Column 2)	Affects Our: (Column 3)
Person, Place or Thing		☐ Self-Esteem ☐ Security ☐ Ambitions ☐ Personal Relations ☐ Sex Relations ☐ Pride/Shame ☐ Fear
Ask Ourselves: ** (AA 67.3) * (AA 62.2)	Putting out of our mind the wrong others had done, we resolutely looked for our own mistakes… We admitted our wrongs honestly…** **STEPS 4** and/or **10** - **(Column 4)**	
Where had I been selfish, self-centred or self-seeking?**		
Where had I been dishonest?**		
Where had I been frightened?**		
For what had I been responsible?**		
What decisions did I make based on self that later placed me in a position to be hurt?*		
When in the past did I make this decision? * (Earliest memory)		
Where was I wrong,** what was my part?		
STEPS 6 & 7 – List of Character Defects				
STEP 9 - Amends				**STEP 8**
				☐ Now ☐ Later ☐ Never

FOUR COLUMN INVENTORY…

COLUMN WORK

Resentment (1) and/or Fear:	The Cause (Column 2)	Affects Our: (Column 3)
Person, Place or Thing		☐ Self-Esteem ☐ Security ☐ Ambitions ☐ Personal Relations ☐ Sex Relations ☐ Pride/Shame ☐ Fear
Ask Ourselves: ** (AA 67.3) * (AA 62.2)	Putting out of our mind the wrong others had done, we resolutely looked for our own mistakes… We admitted our wrongs honestly… ** **STEPS 4** and/or **10** - **(Column 4)**	
Where had I been selfish, self-centred or self-seeking?**		
Where had I been dishonest?**		
Where had I been frightened?**		
For what had I been responsible?**		
What decisions did I make based on self that later placed me in a position to be hurt?*		
When in the past did I make this decision? * (Earliest memory)		
Where was I wrong,** what was my part?		

STEPS 6 & 7 – List of Character Defects

STEP 9 - Amends		STEP 8
		☐ Now ☐ Later ☐ Never

INVENTORY FORMS

Resentment (1) and/or Fear:	The Cause (Column 2)	Affects Our: (Column 3)
Person, Place or Thing		☐ Self-Esteem ☐ Security ☐ Ambitions ☐ Personal Relations ☐ Sex Relations ☐ Pride/Shame ☐ Fear
Ask Ourselves: ** (AA 67.3) * (AA 62.2)	Putting out of our mind the wrong others had done, we resolutely looked for our own mistakes... We admitted our wrongs honestly...** **STEPS 4** and/or **10 - (Column 4)**	
Where had I been selfish, self-centred or self-seeking?**		
Where had I been dishonest?**		
Where had I been frightened?**		
For what had I been responsible?**		
What decisions did I make based on self that later placed me in a position to be hurt?*		
When in the past did I make this decision? * (Earliest memory)		
Where was I wrong,** what was my part?		

STEPS 6 & 7 – List of Character Defects			

STEP 9 - Amends	STEP 8
	☐ Now ☐ Later ☐ Never

86   FOUR COLUMN INVENTORY...

COLUMN WORK

Resentment (1) and/or Fear:	The Cause (Column 2)	Affects Our: (Column 3)
Person, Place or Thing		☐ Self-Esteem ☐ Security ☐ Ambitions ☐ Personal Relations ☐ Sex Relations ☐ Pride/Shame ☐ Fear
Ask Ourselves: ** (AA 67.3) * (AA 62.2)	Putting out of our mind the wrong others had done, we resolutely looked for our own mistakes... We admitted our wrongs honestly... ** **STEPS 4** and/or **10** - **(Column 4)**	
Where had I been selfish, self-centred or self-seeking?**		
Where had I been dishonest?**		
Where had I been frightened?**		
For what had I been responsible?**		
What decisions did I make based on self that later placed me in a position to be hurt?*		
When in the past did I make this decision? * (Earliest memory)		
Where was I wrong,** what was my part?		

STEPS 6 & 7 – List of Character Defects				

STEP 9 - Amends	STEP 8
	☐ Now ☐ Later ☐ Never

INVENTORY FORMS

Resentment (1) and/or Fear:	The Cause (Column 2)	Affects Our: (Column 3)
Person, Place or Thing		☐ Self-Esteem ☐ Security ☐ Ambitions ☐ Personal Relations ☐ Sex Relations ☐ Pride/Shame ☐ Fear
Ask Ourselves: ** (AA 67.3) * (AA 62.2)	Putting out of our mind the wrong others had done, we resolutely looked for our own mistakes... We admitted our wrongs honestly...** **STEPS 4** and/or **10** - **(Column 4)**	
Where had I been selfish, self-centred or self-seeking?**		
Where had I been dishonest?**		
Where had I been frightened?**		
For what had I been responsible?**		
What decisions did I make based on self that later placed me in a position to be hurt?*		
When in the past did I make this decision? * (Earliest memory)		
Where was I wrong,** what was my part?		

STEPS 6 & 7 – List of Character Defects			

STEP 9 - Amends	STEP 8
	☐ Now ☐ Later ☐ Never

COLUMN WORK

Resentment (1) and/or Fear:	The Cause (Column 2)	Affects Our: (Column 3)
Person, Place or Thing		☐ Self-Esteem ☐ Security ☐ Ambitions ☐ Personal Relations ☐ Sex Relations ☐ Pride/Shame ☐ Fear
Ask Ourselves: ** (AA 67.3) * (AA 62.2)	Putting out of our mind the wrong others had done, we resolutely looked for our own mistakes… We admitted our wrongs honestly…** **STEPS 4** and/or **10** - **(Column 4)**	
Where had I been selfish, self-centred or self-seeking?**		
Where had I been dishonest?**		
Where had I been frightened?**		
For what had I been responsible?**		
What decisions did I make based on self that later placed me in a position to be hurt?*		
When in the past did I make this decision? * (Earliest memory)		
Where was I wrong,** what was my part?		
STEPS 6 & 7 – List of Character Defects		
STEP 9 - Amends		**STEP 8**
		☐ Now ☐ Later ☐ Never

FORMS ONLY

INVENTORY FORMS

Resentment (1) and/or Fear:	The Cause (Column 2)	Affects Our: (Column 3)
Person, Place or Thing		☐ Self-Esteem ☐ Security ☐ Ambitions ☐ Personal Relations ☐ Sex Relations ☐ Pride/Shame ☐ Fear
Ask Ourselves: ** (AA 67.3) * (AA 62.2)	Putting out of our mind the wrong others had done, we resolutely looked for our own mistakes... We admitted our wrongs honestly...** **STEPS 4** and/or **10 - (Column 4)**	
Where had I been selfish, self-centred or self-seeking?**		
Where had I been dishonest?**		
Where had I been frightened?**		
For what had I been responsible?**		
What decisions did I make based on self that later placed me in a position to be hurt?*		
When in the past did I make this decision? * (Earliest memory)		
Where was I wrong,** what was my part?		

STEPS 6 & 7 – List of Character Defects

STEP 9 - Amends	STEP 8
	☐ Now ☐ Later ☐ Never

FOUR COLUMN INVENTORY...

COLUMN WORK

Resentment and/or Fear: (1)	The Cause (Column 2)	Affects Our: (Column 3)
Person, Place or Thing		☐ Self-Esteem ☐ Security ☐ Ambitions ☐ Personal Relations ☐ Sex Relations ☐ Pride/Shame ☐ Fear
Ask Ourselves: ** (AA 67.3) * (AA 62.2)	Putting out of our mind the wrong others had done, we resolutely looked for our own mistakes... We admitted our wrongs honestly...** **STEPS 4** and/or **10** - **(Column 4)**	
Where had I been selfish, self-centred or self-seeking?**		
Where had I been dishonest?**		
Where had I been frightened?**		
For what had I been responsible?**		
What decisions did I make based on self that later placed me in a position to be hurt?*		
When in the past did I make this decision? * (Earliest memory)		
Where was I wrong,** what was my part?		

STEPS 6 & 7 – List of Character Defects				

STEP 9 - Amends	STEP 8
	☐ Now ☐ Later ☐ Never

INVENTORY FORMS

Resentment (1) and/or Fear:	The Cause (Column 2)	Affects Our: (Column 3)
Person, Place or Thing		☐ Self-Esteem ☐ Security ☐ Ambitions ☐ Personal Relations ☐ Sex Relations ☐ Pride/Shame ☐ Fear
Ask Ourselves: ** (AA 67.3) * (AA 62.2)	Putting out of our mind the wrong others had done, we resolutely looked for our own mistakes... We admitted our wrongs honestly...** **STEPS 4 and/or 10 - (Column 4)**	
Where had I been selfish, self-centred or self-seeking?**		
Where had I been dishonest?**		
Where had I been frightened?**		
For what had I been responsible?**		
What decisions did I make based on self that later placed me in a position to be hurt?*		
When in the past did I make this decision? * (Earliest memory)		
Where was I wrong,** what was my part?		

STEPS 6 & 7 – List of Character Defects

STEP 9 - Amends	STEP 8
	☐ Now ☐ Later ☐ Never

FOUR COLUMN INVENTORY...

COLUMN WORK

Resentment (1) and/or Fear:	The Cause (Column 2)	Affects Our: (Column 3)
Person, Place or Thing		☐ Self-Esteem ☐ Security ☐ Ambitions ☐ Personal Relations ☐ Sex Relations ☐ Pride/Shame ☐ Fear
Ask Ourselves: ** (AA 67.3) * (AA 62.2)	Putting out of our mind the wrong others had done, we resolutely looked for our own mistakes… We admitted our wrongs honestly…** **STEPS 4 and/or 10 - (Column 4)**	
Where had I been selfish, self-centred or self-seeking?**		
Where had I been dishonest?**		
Where had I been frightened?**		
For what had I been responsible?**		
What decisions did I make based on self that later placed me in a position to be hurt?*		
When in the past did I make this decision? * (Earliest memory)		
Where was I wrong,** what was my part?		

STEPS 6 & 7 – List of Character Defects

STEP 9 - Amends	STEP 8
	☐ Now ☐ Later ☐ Never

FORMS ONLY

INVENTORY FORMS

Resentment (1) and/or Fear:	The Cause (Column 2)	Affects Our: (Column 3)
Person, Place or Thing		☐ Self-Esteem ☐ Security ☐ Ambitions ☐ Personal Relations ☐ Sex Relations ☐ Pride/Shame ☐ Fear
Ask Ourselves: ** (AA 67.3) * (AA 62.2)	Putting out of our mind the wrong others had done, we resolutely looked for our own mistakes... We admitted our wrongs honestly...** **STEPS 4** and/or **10 - (Column 4)**	
Where had I been selfish, self-centred or self-seeking?**		
Where had I been dishonest?**		
Where had I been frightened?**		
For what had I been responsible?**		
What decisions did I make based on self that later placed me in a position to be hurt?*		
When in the past did I make this decision? * (Earliest memory)		
Where was I wrong,** what was my part?		

STEPS 6 & 7 – List of Character Defects			

STEP 9 - Amends		STEP 8
		☐ Now ☐ Later ☐ Never

FOUR COLUMN INVENTORY...

COLUMN WORK

Resentment and/or Fear: (1)	The Cause (Column 2)	Affects Our: (Column 3)
Person, Place or Thing		☐ Self-Esteem ☐ Security ☐ Ambitions ☐ Personal Relations ☐ Sex Relations ☐ Pride/Shame ☐ Fear
Ask Ourselves: ** (AA 67.3) * (AA 62.2)	Putting out of our mind the wrong others had done, we resolutely looked for our own mistakes… We admitted our wrongs honestly…** **STEPS 4 and/or 10 - (Column 4)**	
Where had I been selfish, self-centred or self-seeking?**		
Where had I been dishonest?**		
Where had I been frightened?**		
For what had I been responsible?**		
What decisions did I make based on self that later placed me in a position to be hurt?*		
When in the past did I make this decision? * (Earliest memory)		
Where was I wrong,** what was my part?		

STEPS 6 & 7 – List of Character Defects

STEP 9 - Amends	STEP 8
	☐ Now ☐ Later ☐ Never

INVENTORY FORMS

Resentment (1) and/or Fear:	The Cause (Column 2)	Affects Our: (Column 3)
Person, Place or Thing		☐ Self-Esteem ☐ Security ☐ Ambitions ☐ Personal Relations ☐ Sex Relations ☐ Pride/Shame ☐ Fear
Ask Ourselves: ** (AA 67.3) * (AA 62.2)	Putting out of our mind the wrong others had done, we resolutely looked for our own mistakes... We admitted our wrongs honestly...** **STEPS 4 and/or 10 - (Column 4)**	
Where had I been selfish, self-centred or self-seeking?**		
Where had I been dishonest?**		
Where had I been frightened?**		
For what had I been responsible?**		
What decisions did I make based on self that later placed me in a position to be hurt?*		
When in the past did I make this decision? * (Earliest memory)		
Where was I wrong,** what was my part?		

STEPS 6 & 7 – List of Character Defects			

STEP 9 - Amends	STEP 8
	☐ Now ☐ Later ☐ Never

COLUMN WORK

Resentment (1) and/or Fear:	The Cause (Column 2)	Affects Our: (Column 3)
Person, Place or Thing		☐ Self-Esteem ☐ Security ☐ Ambitions ☐ Personal Relations ☐ Sex Relations ☐ Pride/Shame ☐ Fear
Ask Ourselves: ** (AA 67.3) * (AA 62.2)	Putting out of our mind the wrong others had done, we resolutely looked for our own mistakes… We admitted our wrongs honestly…** **STEPS 4** and/or **10** - **(Column 4)**	
Where had I been selfish, self-centred or self-seeking?**		
Where had I been dishonest?**		
Where had I been frightened?**		
For what had I been responsible?**		
What decisions did I make based on self that later placed me in a position to be hurt?*		
When in the past did I make this decision? * (Earliest memory)		
Where was I wrong,** what was my part?		

STEPS 6 & 7 – List of Character Defects				

STEP 9 - Amends	STEP 8
	☐ Now ☐ Later ☐ Never

FORMS ONLY

INVENTORY FORMS

Resentment (1) and/or Fear:	The Cause (Column 2)	Affects Our: (Column 3)
Person, Place or Thing		☐ Self-Esteem ☐ Security ☐ Ambitions ☐ Personal Relations ☐ Sex Relations ☐ Pride/Shame ☐ Fear
Ask Ourselves: ** (AA 67.3) * (AA 62.2)	Putting out of our mind the wrong others had done, we resolutely looked for our own mistakes... We admitted our wrongs honestly...** **STEPS 4** and/or **10** - **(Column 4)**	
Where had I been selfish, self-centred or self-seeking?**		
Where had I been dishonest?**		
Where had I been frightened?**		
For what had I been responsible?**		
What decisions did I make based on self that later placed me in a position to be hurt?*		
When in the past did I make this decision? * (Earliest memory)		
Where was I wrong,** what was my part?		

STEPS 6 & 7 – List of Character Defects			

STEP 9 - Amends	STEP 8
	☐ Now ☐ Later ☐ Never

FOUR COLUMN INVENTORY...

COLUMN WORK

Resentment (1) and/or Fear:	The Cause (Column 2)	Affects Our: (Column 3)
Person, Place or Thing		☐ Self-Esteem ☐ Security ☐ Ambitions ☐ Personal Relations ☐ Sex Relations ☐ Pride/Shame ☐ Fear
Ask Ourselves: ** (AA 67.3) * (AA 62.2)	Putting out of our mind the wrong others had done, we resolutely looked for our own mistakes… We admitted our wrongs honestly… ** **STEPS 4** and/or **10 - (Column 4)**	
Where had I been selfish, self-centred or self-seeking?**		
Where had I been dishonest?**		
Where had I been frightened?**		
For what had I been responsible?**		
What decisions did I make based on self that later placed me in a position to be hurt?*		
When in the past did I make this decision? * (Earliest memory)		
Where was I wrong,** what was my part?		

STEPS 6 & 7 – List of Character Defects			

STEP 9 - Amends	STEP 8
	☐ Now ☐ Later ☐ Never

FORMS ONLY

INVENTORY FORMS

Resentment (1) and/or Fear:	The Cause (Column 2)	Affects Our: (Column 3)
Person, Place or Thing		☐ Self-Esteem ☐ Security ☐ Ambitions ☐ Personal Relations ☐ Sex Relations ☐ Pride/Shame ☐ Fear
Ask Ourselves: ** (AA 67.3) * (AA 62.2)	Putting out of our mind the wrong others had done, we resolutely looked for our own mistakes... We admitted our wrongs honestly...** **STEPS 4 and/or 10 - (Column 4)**	
Where had I been selfish, self-centred or self-seeking?**		
Where had I been dishonest?**		
Where had I been frightened?**		
For what had I been responsible?**		
What decisions did I make based on self that later placed me in a position to be hurt?*		
When in the past did I make this decision? * (Earliest memory)		
Where was I wrong,** what was my part?		

STEPS 6 & 7 – List of Character Defects			

STEP 9 - Amends	STEP 8
	☐ Now ☐ Later ☐ Never

COLUMN WORK

Resentment (1) and/or Fear:	The Cause (Column 2)	Affects Our: (Column 3)
Person, Place or Thing		☐ Self-Esteem ☐ Security ☐ Ambitions ☐ Personal Relations ☐ Sex Relations ☐ Pride/Shame ☐ Fear
Ask Ourselves: ** (AA 67.3) * (AA 62.2)	Putting out of our mind the wrong others had done, we resolutely looked for our own mistakes... We admitted our wrongs honestly...** **STEPS 4** and/or **10** - **(Column 4)**	
Where had I been selfish, self-centred or self-seeking?**		
Where had I been dishonest?**		
Where had I been frightened?**		
For what had I been responsible?**		
What decisions did I make based on self that later placed me in a position to be hurt?*		
When in the past did I make this decision? * (Earliest memory)		
Where was I wrong,** what was my part?		

STEPS 6 & 7 – List of Character Defects				

STEP 9 - Amends	STEP 8
	☐ Now ☐ Later ☐ Never

FORMS ONLY

INVENTORY FORMS

Resentment (1) and/or Fear:	The Cause (Column 2)	Affects Our: (Column 3)
Person, Place or Thing		❏ Self-Esteem ❏ Security ❏ Ambitions ❏ Personal Relations ❏ Sex Relations ❏ Pride/Shame ❏ Fear
Ask Ourselves: ** (AA 67.3) * (AA 62.2)	Putting out of our mind the wrong others had done, we resolutely looked for our own mistakes… We admitted our wrongs honestly…** **STEPS 4** and/or **10 - (Column 4)**	
Where had I been selfish, self-centred or self-seeking?**		
Where had I been dishonest?**		
Where had I been frightened?**		
For what had I been responsible?**		
What decisions did I make based on self that later placed me in a position to be hurt?*		
When in the past did I make this decision? * (Earliest memory)		
Where was I wrong,** what was my part?		

STEPS 6 & 7 – List of Character Defects			

STEP 9 - Amends	STEP 8
	❏ Now ❏ Later ❏ Never

COLUMN WORK

Resentment (1) and/or Fear:	The Cause (Column 2)	Affects Our: (Column 3)
Person, Place or Thing		☐ Self-Esteem ☐ Security ☐ Ambitions ☐ Personal Relations ☐ Sex Relations ☐ Pride/Shame ☐ Fear
Ask Ourselves: ** (AA 67.3) * (AA 62.2)	Putting out of our mind the wrong others had done, we resolutely looked for our own mistakes… We admitted our wrongs honestly…** **STEPS 4** and/or **10** - **(Column 4)**	
Where had I been selfish, self-centred or self-seeking?**		
Where had I been dishonest?**		
Where had I been frightened?**		
For what had I been responsible?**		
What decisions did I make based on self that later placed me in a position to be hurt?*		
When in the past did I make this decision? * (Earliest memory)		
Where was I wrong,** what was my part?		

STEPS 6 & 7 – List of Character Defects				

STEP 9 - Amends	STEP 8
	☐ Now ☐ Later ☐ Never

FORMS ONLY

INVENTORY FORMS

Resentment (1) and/or Fear:	The Cause (Column 2)	Affects Our: (Column 3)
Person, Place or Thing		❏ Self-Esteem ❏ Security ❏ Ambitions ❏ Personal Relations ❏ Sex Relations ❏ Pride/Shame ❏ Fear
Ask Ourselves: ** (AA 67.3) * (AA 62.2)	Putting out of our mind the wrong others had done, we resolutely looked for our own mistakes... We admitted our wrongs honestly...** **STEPS 4** and/or **10 - (Column 4)**	
Where had I been selfish, self-centred or self-seeking?**		
Where had I been dishonest?**		
Where had I been frightened?**		
For what had I been responsible?**		
What decisions did I make based on self that later placed me in a position to be hurt?*		
When in the past did I make this decision? * (Earliest memory)		
Where was I wrong,** what was my part?		

STEPS 6 & 7 – List of Character Defects				

STEP 9 - Amends	STEP 8
	❏ Now ❏ Later ❏ Never

COLUMN WORK

Resentment (1) and/or Fear:	The Cause (Column 2)	Affects Our: (Column 3)
Person, Place or Thing		☐ Self-Esteem ☐ Security ☐ Ambitions ☐ Personal Relations ☐ Sex Relations ☐ Pride/Shame ☐ Fear
Ask Ourselves: ** (AA 67.3) * (AA 62.2)	Putting out of our mind the wrong others had done, we resolutely looked for our own mistakes… We admitted our wrongs honestly… ** **STEPS 4 and/or 10 - (Column 4)**	
Where had I been selfish, self-centred or self-seeking?**		
Where had I been dishonest?**		
Where had I been frightened?**		
For what had I been responsible?**		
What decisions did I make based on self that later placed me in a position to be hurt?*		
When in the past did I make this decision? * (Earliest memory)		
Where was I wrong,** what was my part?		

STEPS 6 & 7 – List of Character Defects			

STEP 9 - Amends	STEP 8
	☐ Now ☐ Later ☐ Never

FORMS ONLY

INVENTORY FORMS

Resentment (1) and/or Fear:	The Cause (Column 2)	Affects Our: (Column 3)
Person, Place or Thing		☐ Self-Esteem ☐ Security ☐ Ambitions ☐ Personal Relations ☐ Sex Relations ☐ Pride/Shame ☐ Fear
Ask Ourselves: ** (AA 67.3) * (AA 62.2)	Putting out of our mind the wrong others had done, we resolutely looked for our own mistakes... We admitted our wrongs honestly...** **STEPS 4** and/or **10 - (Column 4)**	
Where had I been selfish, self-centred or self-seeking?**		
Where had I been dishonest?**		
Where had I been frightened?**		
For what had I been responsible?**		
What decisions did I make based on self that later placed me in a position to be hurt?*		
When in the past did I make this decision? * (Earliest memory)		
Where was I wrong,** what was my part?		

STEPS 6 & 7 – List of Character Defects			

STEP 9 - Amends	STEP 8
	☐ Now ☐ Later ☐ Never

106   FOUR COLUMN INVENTORY...

COLUMN WORK

Resentment (1) and/or Fear:	The Cause (Column 2)	Affects Our: (Column 3)
Person, Place or Thing		☐ Self-Esteem ☐ Security ☐ Ambitions ☐ Personal Relations ☐ Sex Relations ☐ Pride/Shame ☐ Fear
Ask Ourselves: ** (AA 67.3) * (AA 62.2)	Putting out of our mind the wrong others had done, we resolutely looked for our own mistakes... We admitted our wrongs honestly...** **STEPS 4** and/or **10** - **(Column 4)**	
Where had I been selfish, self-centred or self-seeking?**		
Where had I been dishonest?**		
Where had I been frightened?**		
For what had I been responsible?**		
What decisions did I make based on self that later placed me in a position to be hurt?*		
When in the past did I make this decision? * (Earliest memory)		
Where was I wrong,** what was my part?		

STEPS 6 & 7 – List of Character Defects				

STEP 9 - Amends	STEP 8
	☐ Now ☐ Later ☐ Never

FORMS ONLY

INVENTORY FORMS

Resentment (1) and/or Fear:	The Cause (Column 2)	Affects Our: (Column 3)
Person, Place or Thing		☐ Self-Esteem ☐ Security ☐ Ambitions ☐ Personal Relations ☐ Sex Relations ☐ Pride/Shame ☐ Fear
Ask Ourselves: ** (AA 67.3) * (AA 62.2)	Putting out of our mind the wrong others had done, we resolutely looked for our own mistakes... We admitted our wrongs honestly...** **STEPS 4** and/or **10** - **(Column 4)**	
Where had I been selfish, self-centred or self-seeking?**		
Where had I been dishonest?**		
Where had I been frightened?**		
For what had I been responsible?**		
What decisions did I make based on self that later placed me in a position to be hurt?*		
When in the past did I make this decision? * (Earliest memory)		
Where was I wrong,** what was my part?		

STEPS 6 & 7 – List of Character Defects			

STEP 9 - Amends	STEP 8
	☐ Now ☐ Later ☐ Never

FOUR COLUMN INVENTORY...

COLUMN WORK

Resentment (1) and/or Fear:	The Cause (Column 2)	Affects Our: (Column 3)
Person, Place or Thing		☐ Self-Esteem ☐ Security ☐ Ambitions ☐ Personal Relations ☐ Sex Relations ☐ Pride/Shame ☐ Fear
Ask Ourselves: ** (AA 67.3) * (AA 62.2)	Putting out of our mind the wrong others had done, we resolutely looked for our own mistakes... We admitted our wrongs honestly...** **STEPS 4** and/or **10** - **(Column 4)**	
Where had I been selfish, self-centred or self-seeking?**		
Where had I been dishonest?**		
Where had I been frightened?**		
For what had I been responsible?**		
What decisions did I make based on self that later placed me in a position to be hurt?*		
When in the past did I make this decision? * (Earliest memory)		
Where was I wrong,** what was my part?		

STEPS 6 & 7 – List of Character Defects				

STEP 9 - Amends	STEP 8
	☐ Now ☐ Later ☐ Never

FORMS ONLY

INVENTORY FORMS

Resentment (1) and/or Fear:	The Cause (Column 2)	Affects Our: (Column 3)
Person, Place or Thing		☐ Self-Esteem ☐ Security ☐ Ambitions ☐ Personal Relations ☐ Sex Relations ☐ Pride/Shame ☐ Fear
Ask Ourselves: ** (AA 67.3) * (AA 62.2)	Putting out of our mind the wrong others had done, we resolutely looked for our own mistakes... We admitted our wrongs honestly...** **STEPS 4** and/or **10** - **(Column 4)**	
Where had I been selfish, self-centred or self-seeking?**		
Where had I been dishonest?**		
Where had I been frightened?**		
For what had I been responsible?**		
What decisions did I make based on self that later placed me in a position to be hurt?*		
When in the past did I make this decision? * (Earliest memory)		
Where was I wrong,** what was my part?		

STEPS 6 & 7 – List of Character Defects				

STEP 9 - Amends	STEP 8
	☐ Now ☐ Later ☐ Never

FOUR COLUMN INVENTORY...

COLUMN WORK

Resentment and/or Fear: (1)	The Cause (Column 2)	Affects Our: (Column 3)
Person, Place or Thing		☐ Self-Esteem ☐ Security ☐ Ambitions ☐ Personal Relations ☐ Sex Relations ☐ Pride/Shame ☐ Fear
Ask Ourselves: ** (AA 67.3) * (AA 62.2)	Putting out of our mind the wrong others had done, we resolutely looked for our own mistakes… We admitted our wrongs honestly… ** **STEPS 4 and/or 10 - (Column 4)**	
Where had I been selfish, self-centred or self-seeking?**		
Where had I been dishonest?**		
Where had I been frightened?**		
For what had I been responsible?**		
What decisions did I make based on self that later placed me in a position to be hurt?*		
When in the past did I make this decision? * (Earliest memory)		
Where was I wrong,** what was my part?		
STEPS 6 & 7 – List of Character Defects		

STEP 9 - Amends		STEP 8
		☐ Now ☐ Later ☐ Never

FORMS ONLY

INVENTORY FORMS

Resentment (1) and/or Fear:	The Cause (Column 2)	Affects Our: (Column 3)
Person, Place or Thing		☐ Self-Esteem ☐ Security ☐ Ambitions ☐ Personal Relations ☐ Sex Relations ☐ Pride/Shame ☐ Fear
Ask Ourselves: ** (AA 67.3) * (AA 62.2)	Putting out of our mind the wrong others had done, we resolutely looked for our own mistakes... We admitted our wrongs honestly...** **STEPS 4 and/or 10 - (Column 4)**	
Where had I been selfish, self-centred or self-seeking?**		
Where had I been dishonest?**		
Where had I been frightened?**		
For what had I been responsible?**		
What decisions did I make based on self that later placed me in a position to be hurt?*		
When in the past did I make this decision? * (Earliest memory)		
Where was I wrong,** what was my part?		
STEPS 6 & 7 – List of Character Defects		

STEP 9 - Amends	STEP 8
	☐ Now ☐ Later ☐ Never

COLUMN WORK

Resentment and/or Fear: (1)	The Cause (Column 2)	Affects Our: (Column 3)
Person, Place or Thing		☐ Self-Esteem ☐ Security ☐ Ambitions ☐ Personal Relations ☐ Sex Relations ☐ Pride/Shame ☐ Fear
Ask Ourselves: ** (AA 67.3) * (AA 62.2)	Putting out of our mind the wrong others had done, we resolutely looked for our own mistakes… We admitted our wrongs honestly… ** **STEPS 4** and/or **10 - (Column 4)**	
Where had I been selfish, self-centred or self-seeking?**		
Where had I been dishonest?**		
Where had I been frightened?**		
For what had I been responsible?**		
What decisions did I make based on self that later placed me in a position to be hurt?*		
When in the past did I make this decision? * (Earliest memory)		
Where was I wrong,** what was my part?		

STEPS 6 & 7 – List of Character Defects				

STEP 9 - Amends	STEP 8
	☐ Now ☐ Later ☐ Never

FORMS ONLY

INVENTORY FORMS

Resentment (1) and/or Fear:	The Cause (Column 2)	Affects Our: (Column 3)
Person, Place or Thing		☐ Self-Esteem ☐ Security ☐ Ambitions ☐ Personal Relations ☐ Sex Relations ☐ Pride/Shame ☐ Fear
Ask Ourselves: ** (AA 67.3) * (AA 62.2)	Putting out of our mind the wrong others had done, we resolutely looked for our own mistakes... We admitted our wrongs honestly...** **STEPS 4** and/or **10 - (Column 4)**	
Where had I been selfish, self-centred or self-seeking?**		
Where had I been dishonest?**		
Where had I been frightened?**		
For what had I been responsible?**		
What decisions did I make based on self that later placed me in a position to be hurt?*		
When in the past did I make this decision? * (Earliest memory)		
Where was I wrong,** what was my part?		

STEPS 6 & 7 – List of Character Defects

STEP 9 - Amends	STEP 8
	☐ Now ☐ Later ☐ Never

COLUMN WORK

Resentment (1) and/or Fear:	The Cause (Column 2)	Affects Our: (Column 3)
Person, Place or Thing		☐ Self-Esteem ☐ Security ☐ Ambitions ☐ Personal Relations ☐ Sex Relations ☐ Pride/Shame ☐ Fear
Ask Ourselves: ** (AA 67.3) * (AA 62.2)	Putting out of our mind the wrong others had done, we resolutely looked for our own mistakes… We admitted our wrongs honestly…** **STEPS 4** and/or **10** - **(Column 4)**	
Where had I been selfish, self-centred or self-seeking?**		
Where had I been dishonest?**		
Where had I been frightened?**		
For what had I been responsible?**		
What decisions did I make based on self that later placed me in a position to be hurt?*		
When in the past did I make this decision? * (Earliest memory)		
Where was I wrong,** what was my part?		

STEPS 6 & 7 – List of Character Defects				

STEP 9 - Amends	STEP 8
	☐ Now ☐ Later ☐ Never

FORMS ONLY

INVENTORY FORMS

Resentment (1) and/or Fear:	The Cause (Column 2)	Affects Our: (Column 3)
Person, Place or Thing		☐ Self-Esteem ☐ Security ☐ Ambitions ☐ Personal Relations ☐ Sex Relations ☐ Pride/Shame ☐ Fear
Ask Ourselves: ** (AA 67.3) * (AA 62.2)	Putting out of our mind the wrong others had done, we resolutely looked for our own mistakes... We admitted our wrongs honestly...** **STEPS 4** and/or **10** - **(Column 4)**	
Where had I been selfish, self-centred or self-seeking?**		
Where had I been dishonest?**		
Where had I been frightened?**		
For what had I been responsible?**		
What decisions did I make based on self that later placed me in a position to be hurt?*		
When in the past did I make this decision? * (Earliest memory)		
Where was I wrong,** what was my part?		
STEPS 6 & 7 – List of Character Defects				
STEP 9 - Amends		**STEP 8**
		☐ Now ☐ Later ☐ Never

COLUMN WORK

Resentment and/or Fear: (1)	The Cause (Column 2)	Affects Our: (Column 3)
Person, Place or Thing		☐ Self-Esteem ☐ Security ☐ Ambitions ☐ Personal Relations ☐ Sex Relations ☐ Pride/Shame ☐ Fear
Ask Ourselves: ** (AA 67.3) * (AA 62.2)	Putting out of our mind the wrong others had done, we resolutely looked for our own mistakes... We admitted our wrongs honestly...** **STEPS 4** and/or **10** - **(Column 4)**	
Where had I been selfish, self-centred or self-seeking?**		
Where had I been dishonest?**		
Where had I been frightened?**		
For what had I been responsible?**		
What decisions did I make based on self that later placed me in a position to be hurt?*		
When in the past did I make this decision? * (Earliest memory)		
Where was I wrong,** what was my part?		

STEPS 6 & 7 – List of Character Defects

STEP 9 - Amends	STEP 8
	☐ **Now** ☐ **Later** ☐ **Never**

FORMS ONLY

INVENTORY FORMS

Resentment (1) and/or Fear:	The Cause (Column 2)	Affects Our: (Column 3)
Person, Place or Thing		☐ Self-Esteem ☐ Security ☐ Ambitions ☐ Personal Relations ☐ Sex Relations ☐ Pride/Shame ☐ Fear
Ask Ourselves: ** (AA 67.3) * (AA 62.2)	Putting out of our mind the wrong others had done, we resolutely looked for our own mistakes… We admitted our wrongs honestly…** **STEPS 4** and/or **10 - (Column 4)**	
Where had I been selfish, self-centred or self-seeking?**		
Where had I been dishonest?**		
Where had I been frightened?**		
For what had I been responsible?**		
What decisions did I make based on self that later placed me in a position to be hurt?*		
When in the past did I make this decision? * (Earliest memory)		
Where was I wrong,** what was my part?		

STEPS 6 & 7 – List of Character Defects			

STEP 9 - Amends	STEP 8
	☐ Now ☐ Later ☐ Never

COLUMN WORK

Resentment (1) and/or Fear:	The Cause (Column 2)	Affects Our: (Column 3)
Person, Place or Thing		☐ Self-Esteem ☐ Security ☐ Ambitions ☐ Personal Relations ☐ Sex Relations ☐ Pride/Shame ☐ Fear
Ask Ourselves: ** (AA 67.3) * (AA 62.2)	Putting out of our mind the wrong others had done, we resolutely looked for our own mistakes… We admitted our wrongs honestly…** **STEPS 4** and/or **10 - (Column 4)**	
Where had I been selfish, self-centred or self-seeking?**		
Where had I been dishonest?**		
Where had I been frightened?**		
For what had I been responsible?**		
What decisions did I make based on self that later placed me in a position to be hurt?*		
When in the past did I make this decision? * (Earliest memory)		
Where was I wrong,** what was my part?		

STEPS 6 & 7 – List of Character Defects

STEP 9 - Amends	STEP 8
	☐ Now ☐ Later ☐ Never

FORMS ONLY

INVENTORY FORMS

Resentment (1) and/or Fear:	The Cause (Column 2)	Affects Our: (Column 3)
Person, Place or Thing		☐ Self-Esteem ☐ Security ☐ Ambitions ☐ Personal Relations ☐ Sex Relations ☐ Pride/Shame ☐ Fear
Ask Ourselves: ** (AA 67.3) * (AA 62.2)	Putting out of our mind the wrong others had done, we resolutely looked for our own mistakes... We admitted our wrongs honestly...** **STEPS 4** and/or **10 - (Column 4)**	
Where had I been selfish, self-centred or self-seeking?**		
Where had I been dishonest?**		
Where had I been frightened?**		
For what had I been responsible?**		
What decisions did I make based on self that later placed me in a position to be hurt?*		
When in the past did I make this decision? * (Earliest memory)		
Where was I wrong,** what was my part?		

STEPS 6 & 7 – List of Character Defects			

STEP 9 - Amends	STEP 8
	☐ Now ☐ Later ☐ Never

FOUR COLUMN INVENTORY...

COLUMN WORK

Resentment (1) and/or Fear:	The Cause (Column 2)	Affects Our: (Column 3)
Person, Place or Thing		☐ Self-Esteem ☐ Security ☐ Ambitions ☐ Personal Relations ☐ Sex Relations ☐ Pride/Shame ☐ Fear
Ask Ourselves: ** (AA 67.3) * (AA 62.2)	Putting out of our mind the wrong others had done, we resolutely looked for our own mistakes... We admitted our wrongs honestly...** **STEPS 4 and/or 10 - (Column 4)**	
Where had I been selfish, self-centred or self-seeking?**		
Where had I been dishonest?**		
Where had I been frightened?**		
For what had I been responsible?**		
What decisions did I make based on self that later placed me in a position to be hurt?*		
When in the past did I make this decision? * (Earliest memory)		
Where was I wrong,** what was my part?		

STEPS 6 & 7 – List of Character Defects			

STEP 9 - Amends	STEP 8
	☐ Now ☐ Later ☐ Never

FORMS ONLY

INVENTORY FORMS

Resentment (1) and/or Fear:	The Cause (Column 2)	Affects Our: (Column 3)
Person, Place or Thing		☐ Self-Esteem ☐ Security ☐ Ambitions ☐ Personal Relations ☐ Sex Relations ☐ Pride/Shame ☐ Fear
Ask Ourselves: ** (AA 67.3) * (AA 62.2)	Putting out of our mind the wrong others had done, we resolutely looked for our own mistakes… We admitted our wrongs honestly…** **STEPS 4** and/or **10 - (Column 4)**	
Where had I been selfish, self-centred or self-seeking?**		
Where had I been dishonest?**		
Where had I been frightened?**		
For what had I been responsible?**		
What decisions did I make based on self that later placed me in a position to be hurt?*		
When in the past did I make this decision? * (Earliest memory)		
Where was I wrong,** what was my part?		
STEPS 6 & 7 – List of Character Defects			
STEP 9 - Amends			**STEP 8**
			☐ Now ☐ Later ☐ Never

FOUR COLUMN INVENTORY…

COLUMN WORK

Resentment (1) and/or Fear:	The Cause (Column 2)	Affects Our: (Column 3)
Person, Place or Thing		☐ Self-Esteem ☐ Security ☐ Ambitions ☐ Personal Relations ☐ Sex Relations ☐ Pride/Shame ☐ Fear
Ask Ourselves: ** (AA 67.3) * (AA 62.2)	Putting out of our mind the wrong others had done, we resolutely looked for our own mistakes… We admitted our wrongs honestly…** STEPS 4 and/or 10 - (Column 4)	
Where had I been selfish, self-centred or self-seeking?**		
Where had I been dishonest?**		
Where had I been frightened?**		
For what had I been responsible?**		
What decisions did I make based on self that later placed me in a position to be hurt?*		
When in the past did I make this decision? * (Earliest memory)		
Where was I wrong,** what was my part?		

STEPS 6 & 7 – List of Character Defects				

STEP 9 - Amends	STEP 8
	☐ Now ☐ Later ☐ Never

FORMS ONLY

INVENTORY FORMS

Resentment (1) and/or Fear:	The Cause (Column 2)	Affects Our: (Column 3)
Person, Place or Thing		☐ Self-Esteem ☐ Security ☐ Ambitions ☐ Personal Relations ☐ Sex Relations ☐ Pride/Shame ☐ Fear
Ask Ourselves: ** (AA 67.3) * (AA 62.2)	Putting out of our mind the wrong others had done, we resolutely looked for our own mistakes… We admitted our wrongs honestly… ** **STEPS 4 and/or 10 - (Column 4)**	
Where had I been selfish, self-centred or self-seeking?**		
Where had I been dishonest?**		
Where had I been frightened?**		
For what had I been responsible?**		
What decisions did I make based on self that later placed me in a position to be hurt?*		
When in the past did I make this decision? * (Earliest memory)		
Where was I wrong,** what was my part?		

STEPS 6 & 7 – List of Character Defects				

STEP 9 - Amends	STEP 8
	☐ Now ☐ Later ☐ Never

FOUR COLUMN INVENTORY…

COLUMN WORK

Resentment (1) and/or Fear:	The Cause (Column 2)	Affects Our: (Column 3)
Person, Place or Thing		☐ Self-Esteem ☐ Security ☐ Ambitions ☐ Personal Relations ☐ Sex Relations ☐ Pride/Shame ☐ Fear
Ask Ourselves: ** (AA 67.3) * (AA 62.2)	Putting out of our mind the wrong others had done, we resolutely looked for our own mistakes... We admitted our wrongs honestly...** **STEPS 4** and/or **10 - (Column 4)**	
Where had I been selfish, self-centred or self-seeking?**		
Where had I been dishonest?**		
Where had I been frightened?**		
For what had I been responsible?**		
What decisions did I make based on self that later placed me in a position to be hurt?*		
When in the past did I make this decision? * (Earliest memory)		
Where was I wrong,** what was my part?		

STEPS 6 & 7 – List of Character Defects			

STEP 9 - Amends	STEP 8
	☐ Now ☐ Later ☐ Never

INVENTORY FORMS

Resentment (1) and/or Fear:	The Cause (Column 2)	Affects Our: (Column 3)
Person, Place or Thing		☐ Self-Esteem ☐ Security ☐ Ambitions ☐ Personal Relations ☐ Sex Relations ☐ Pride/Shame ☐ Fear
Ask Ourselves: ** (AA 67.3) * (AA 62.2)	Putting out of our mind the wrong others had done, we resolutely looked for our own mistakes... We admitted our wrongs honestly...** **STEPS 4** and/or **10** - **(Column 4)**	
Where had I been selfish, self-centred or self-seeking?**		
Where had I been dishonest?**		
Where had I been frightened?**		
For what had I been responsible?**		
What decisions did I make based on self that later placed me in a position to be hurt?*		
When in the past did I make this decision? * (Earliest memory)		
Where was I wrong,** what was my part?		
STEPS 6 & 7 – List of Character Defects		
STEP 9 - Amends		**STEP 8**
		☐ Now ☐ Later ☐ Never

COLUMN WORK

Resentment (1) and/or Fear:	The Cause (Column 2)	Affects Our: (Column 3)
Person, Place or Thing		☐ Self-Esteem ☐ Security ☐ Ambitions ☐ Personal Relations ☐ Sex Relations ☐ Pride/Shame ☐ Fear
Ask Ourselves: ** (AA 67.3) * (AA 62.2)	Putting out of our mind the wrong others had done, we resolutely looked for our own mistakes… We admitted our wrongs honestly… ** **STEPS 4** and/or **10** - **(Column 4)**	
Where had I been selfish, self-centred or self-seeking?**		
Where had I been dishonest?**		
Where had I been frightened?**		
For what had I been responsible?**		
What decisions did I make based on self that later placed me in a position to be hurt?*		
When in the past did I make this decision? * (Earliest memory)		
Where was I wrong,** what was my part?		

STEPS 6 & 7 – List of Character Defects				

STEP 9 - Amends	STEP 8
	☐ Now ☐ Later ☐ Never

FORMS ONLY

INVENTORY FORMS

Resentment (1) and/or Fear:	The Cause (Column 2)	Affects Our: (Column 3)
Person, Place or Thing		☐ Self-Esteem ☐ Security ☐ Ambitions ☐ Personal Relations ☐ Sex Relations ☐ Pride/Shame ☐ Fear
Ask Ourselves: ** (AA 67.3) * (AA 62.2)	Putting out of our mind the wrong others had done, we resolutely looked for our own mistakes... We admitted our wrongs honestly...** **STEPS 4** and/or **10 - (Column 4)**	
Where had I been selfish, self-centred or self-seeking?**		
Where had I been dishonest?**		
Where had I been frightened?**		
For what had I been responsible?**		
What decisions did I make based on self that later placed me in a position to be hurt?*		
When in the past did I make this decision? * (Earliest memory)		
Where was I wrong,** what was my part?		

STEPS 6 & 7 – List of Character Defects			

STEP 9 - Amends	STEP 8
	☐ Now ☐ Later ☐ Never

COLUMN WORK

Resentment and/or Fear: (1)	The Cause (Column 2)	Affects Our: (Column 3)
Person, Place or Thing		☐ Self-Esteem ☐ Security ☐ Ambitions ☐ Personal Relations ☐ Sex Relations ☐ Pride/Shame ☐ Fear
Ask Ourselves: ** (AA 67.3) * (AA 62.2)	Putting out of our mind the wrong others had done, we resolutely looked for our own mistakes… We admitted our wrongs honestly…** **STEPS 4** and/or **10** - **(Column 4)**	
Where had I been selfish, self-centred or self-seeking?**		
Where had I been dishonest?**		
Where had I been frightened?**		
For what had I been responsible?**		
What decisions did I make based on self that later placed me in a position to be hurt?*		
When in the past did I make this decision? * (Earliest memory)		
Where was I wrong,** what was my part?		

STEPS 6 & 7 – List of Character Defects				

STEP 9 - Amends	STEP 8
	☐ Now ☐ Later ☐ Never

INVENTORY FORMS

Resentment (1) and/or Fear:	The Cause (Column 2)	Affects Our: (Column 3)
Person, Place or Thing		☐ Self-Esteem ☐ Security ☐ Ambitions ☐ Personal Relations ☐ Sex Relations ☐ Pride/Shame ☐ Fear
Ask Ourselves: ** (AA 67.3) * (AA 62.2)	Putting out of our mind the wrong others had done, we resolutely looked for our own mistakes… We admitted our wrongs honestly…** **STEPS 4** and/or **10** - **(Column 4)**	
Where had I been selfish, self-centred or self-seeking?**		
Where had I been dishonest?**		
Where had I been frightened?**		
For what had I been responsible?**		
What decisions did I make based on self that later placed me in a position to be hurt?*		
When in the past did I make this decision? * (Earliest memory)		
Where was I wrong,** what was my part?		

STEPS 6 & 7 – List of Character Defects			

STEP 9 - Amends	STEP 8
	☐ Now ☐ Later ☐ Never

FOUR COLUMN INVENTORY…

COLUMN WORK

Resentment and/or Fear: (1)	The Cause (Column 2)	Affects Our: (Column 3)
Person, Place or Thing		☐ Self-Esteem ☐ Security ☐ Ambitions ☐ Personal Relations ☐ Sex Relations ☐ Pride/Shame ☐ Fear
Ask Ourselves: ** (AA 67.3) * (AA 62.2)	Putting out of our mind the wrong others had done, we resolutely looked for our own mistakes... We admitted our wrongs honestly...** STEPS 4 and/or **10** - **(Column 4)**	
Where had I been selfish, self-centred or self-seeking?**		
Where had I been dishonest?**		
Where had I been frightened?**		
For what had I been responsible?**		
What decisions did I make based on self that later placed me in a position to be hurt?*		
When in the past did I make this decision? * (Earliest memory)		
Where was I wrong,** what was my part?		

STEPS 6 & 7 – List of Character Defects

STEP 9 - Amends		STEP 8
		☐ Now ☐ Later ☐ Never

FORMS ONLY

INVENTORY FORMS

Resentment (1) and/or Fear:	The Cause (Column 2)	Affects Our: (Column 3)
Person, Place or Thing		☐ Self-Esteem ☐ Security ☐ Ambitions ☐ Personal Relations ☐ Sex Relations ☐ Pride/Shame ☐ Fear
Ask Ourselves: ** (AA 67.3) * (AA 62.2)	Putting out of our mind the wrong others had done, we resolutely looked for our own mistakes... We admitted our wrongs honestly... ** STEPS 4 and/or 10 - (Column 4)	
Where had I been selfish, self-centred or self-seeking?**		
Where had I been dishonest?**		
Where had I been frightened?**		
For what had I been responsible?**		
What decisions did I make based on self that later placed me in a position to be hurt?*		
When in the past did I make this decision? * (Earliest memory)		
Where was I wrong,** what was my part?		

STEPS 6 & 7 – List of Character Defects

STEP 9 - Amends	STEP 8
	☐ Now ☐ Later ☐ Never

FOUR COLUMN INVENTORY...

COLUMN WORK

Resentment (1) and/or Fear:	The Cause (Column 2)	Affects Our: (Column 3)
Person, Place or Thing		❑ Self-Esteem ❑ Security ❑ Ambitions ❑ Personal Relations ❑ Sex Relations ❑ Pride/Shame ❑ Fear
Ask Ourselves: ** (AA 67.3) * (AA 62.2)	Putting out of our mind the wrong others had done, we resolutely looked for our own mistakes... We admitted our wrongs honestly...** **STEPS 4 and/or 10 - (Column 4)**	
Where had I been selfish, self-centred or self-seeking?**		
Where had I been dishonest?**		
Where had I been frightened?**		
For what had I been responsible?**		
What decisions did I make based on self that later placed me in a position to be hurt?*		
When in the past did I make this decision? * (Earliest memory)		
Where was I wrong,** what was my part?		

STEPS 6 & 7 – List of Character Defects

STEP 9 - Amends | STEP 8

	❑ Now ❑ Later ❑ Never

FORMS ONLY

INVENTORY FORMS

Resentment (1) and/or Fear:	The Cause (Column 2)	Affects Our: (Column 3)
Person, Place or Thing		☐ Self-Esteem ☐ Security ☐ Ambitions ☐ Personal Relations ☐ Sex Relations ☐ Pride/Shame ☐ Fear
Ask Ourselves: ** (AA 67.3) * (AA 62.2)	Putting out of our mind the wrong others had done, we resolutely looked for our own mistakes... We admitted our wrongs honestly...** **STEPS 4 and/or 10 - (Column 4)**	
Where had I been selfish, self-centred or self-seeking?**		
Where had I been dishonest?**		
Where had I been frightened?**		
For what had I been responsible?**		
What decisions did I make based on self that later placed me in a position to be hurt?*		
When in the past did I make this decision? * (Earliest memory)		
Where was I wrong,** what was my part?		

STEPS 6 & 7 – List of Character Defects

STEP 9 - Amends	STEP 8
	☐ Now ☐ Later ☐ Never

FOUR COLUMN INVENTORY...

COLUMN WORK

Resentment and/or Fear: (1)	The Cause (Column 2)	Affects Our: (Column 3)
Person, Place or Thing		☐ Self-Esteem ☐ Security ☐ Ambitions ☐ Personal Relations ☐ Sex Relations ☐ Pride/Shame ☐ Fear
Ask Ourselves: ** (AA 67.3) * (AA 62.2)	Putting out of our mind the wrong others had done, we resolutely looked for our own mistakes... We admitted our wrongs honestly... ** **STEPS 4 and/or 10 - (Column 4)**	
Where had I been selfish, self-centred or self-seeking?**		
Where had I been dishonest?**		
Where had I been frightened?**		
For what had I been responsible?**		
What decisions did I make based on self that later placed me in a position to be hurt?*		
When in the past did I make this decision? * (Earliest memory)		
Where was I wrong,** what was my part?		

STEPS 6 & 7 – List of Character Defects			

STEP 9 - Amends	STEP 8
	☐ Now ☐ Later ☐ Never

FORMS ONLY

INVENTORY FORMS

Resentment (1) and/or Fear:	The Cause (Column 2)	Affects Our: (Column 3)
Person, Place or Thing		☐ Self-Esteem ☐ Security ☐ Ambitions ☐ Personal Relations ☐ Sex Relations ☐ Pride/Shame ☐ Fear
Ask Ourselves: ** (AA 67.3) * (AA 62.2)	Putting out of our mind the wrong others had done, we resolutely looked for our own mistakes... We admitted our wrongs honestly...** **STEPS 4** and/or **10 - (Column 4)**	
Where had I been selfish, self-centred or self-seeking?**		
Where had I been dishonest?**		
Where had I been frightened?**		
For what had I been responsible?**		
What decisions did I make based on self that later placed me in a position to be hurt?*		
When in the past did I make this decision? * (Earliest memory)		
Where was I wrong,** what was my part?		

STEPS 6 & 7 – List of Character Defects			

STEP 9 - Amends	STEP 8
	☐ Now ☐ Later ☐ Never

COLUMN WORK

Resentment (1) and/or Fear:	The Cause (Column 2)	Affects Our: (Column 3)
Person, Place or Thing		☐ Self-Esteem ☐ Security ☐ Ambitions ☐ Personal Relations ☐ Sex Relations ☐ Pride/Shame ☐ Fear
Ask Ourselves: ** (AA 67.3) * (AA 62.2)	Putting out of our mind the wrong others had done, we resolutely looked for our own mistakes... We admitted our wrongs honestly...** **STEPS 4** and/or **10 - (Column 4)**	
Where had I been selfish, self-centred or self-seeking?**		
Where had I been dishonest?**		
Where had I been frightened?**		
For what had I been responsible?**		
What decisions did I make based on self that later placed me in a position to be hurt?*		
When in the past did I make this decision? * (Earliest memory)		
Where was I wrong,** what was my part?		

STEPS 6 & 7 – List of Character Defects				

STEP 9 - Amends	STEP 8
	☐ Now ☐ Later ☐ Never

FORMS ONLY

INVENTORY FORMS

Resentment (1) and/or Fear:	The Cause (Column 2)	Affects Our: (Column 3)
Person, Place or Thing		☐ Self-Esteem ☐ Security ☐ Ambitions ☐ Personal Relations ☐ Sex Relations ☐ Pride/Shame ☐ Fear
Ask Ourselves: ** (AA 67.3) * (AA 62.2)	Putting out of our mind the wrong others had done, we resolutely looked for our own mistakes... We admitted our wrongs honestly...** **STEPS 4 and/or 10 - (Column 4)**	
Where had I been selfish, self-centred or self-seeking?**		
Where had I been dishonest?**		
Where had I been frightened?**		
For what had I been responsible?**		
What decisions did I make based on self that later placed me in a position to be hurt?*		
When in the past did I make this decision? * (Earliest memory)		
Where was I wrong,** what was my part?		

STEPS 6 & 7 – List of Character Defects			

STEP 9 - Amends		STEP 8
		☐ **Now** ☐ **Later** ☐ **Never**

COLUMN WORK

Resentment (1) and/or Fear:	The Cause (Column 2)	Affects Our: (Column 3)
Person, Place or Thing		☐ Self-Esteem ☐ Security ☐ Ambitions ☐ Personal Relations ☐ Sex Relations ☐ Pride/Shame ☐ Fear
Ask Ourselves: ** (AA 67.3) * (AA 62.2)	Putting out of our mind the wrong others had done, we resolutely looked for our own mistakes… We admitted our wrongs honestly…** **STEPS 4** and/or **10** - **(Column 4)**	
Where had I been selfish, self-centred or self-seeking?**		
Where had I been dishonest?**		
Where had I been frightened?**		
For what had I been responsible?**		
What decisions did I make based on self that later placed me in a position to be hurt?*		
When in the past did I make this decision? * (Earliest memory)		
Where was I wrong,** what was my part?		

STEPS 6 & 7 – List of Character Defects					

STEP 9 - Amends	STEP 8
	☐ Now ☐ Later ☐ Never

FORMS ONLY

INVENTORY FORMS

Resentment (1) and/or Fear:	The Cause (Column 2)	Affects Our: (Column 3)
Person, Place or Thing		☐ Self-Esteem ☐ Security ☐ Ambitions ☐ Personal Relations ☐ Sex Relations ☐ Pride/Shame ☐ Fear
Ask Ourselves: ** (AA 67.3) * (AA 62.2)	Putting out of our mind the wrong others had done, we resolutely looked for our own mistakes… We admitted our wrongs honestly…** **STEPS 4** and/or **10** - **(Column 4)**	
Where had I been selfish, self-centred or self-seeking?**		
Where had I been dishonest?**		
Where had I been frightened?**		
For what had I been responsible?**		
What decisions did I make based on self that later placed me in a position to be hurt?*		
When in the past did I make this decision? * (Earliest memory)		
Where was I wrong,** what was my part?		

STEPS 6 & 7 – List of Character Defects			

STEP 9 - Amends	STEP 8
	☐ Now ☐ Later ☐ Never

COLUMN WORK

Resentment (1) and/or Fear:	The Cause (Column 2)	Affects Our: (Column 3)
Person, Place or Thing		☐ Self-Esteem ☐ Security ☐ Ambitions ☐ Personal Relations ☐ Sex Relations ☐ Pride/Shame ☐ Fear
Ask Ourselves: ** (AA 67.3) * (AA 62.2)	Putting out of our mind the wrong others had done, we resolutely looked for our own mistakes… We admitted our wrongs honestly…** **STEPS 4** and/or **10 - (Column 4)**	
Where had I been selfish, self-centred or self-seeking?**		
Where had I been dishonest?**		
Where had I been frightened?**		
For what had I been responsible?**		
What decisions did I make based on self that later placed me in a position to be hurt?*		
When in the past did I make this decision? * (Earliest memory)		
Where was I wrong,** what was my part?		

STEPS 6 & 7 – List of Character Defects			

STEP 9 - Amends	STEP 8
	☐ **Now** ☐ **Later** ☐ **Never**

FORMS ONLY

INVENTORY FORMS

Resentment (1) and/or Fear:	The Cause (Column 2)	Affects Our: (Column 3)
Person, Place or Thing		☐ Self-Esteem ☐ Security ☐ Ambitions ☐ Personal Relations ☐ Sex Relations ☐ Pride/Shame ☐ Fear
Ask Ourselves: ** (AA 67.3) * (AA 62.2)	Putting out of our mind the wrong others had done, we resolutely looked for our own mistakes... We admitted our wrongs honestly...** **STEPS 4 and/or 10 - (Column 4)**	
Where had I been selfish, self-centred or self-seeking?**		
Where had I been dishonest?**		
Where had I been frightened?**		
For what had I been responsible?**		
What decisions did I make based on self that later placed me in a position to be hurt?*		
When in the past did I make this decision? * (Earliest memory)		
Where was I wrong,** what was my part?		

STEPS 6 & 7 – List of Character Defects			

STEP 9 - Amends	STEP 8
	☐ Now ☐ Later ☐ Never

COLUMN WORK

Resentment (1) and/or Fear:	The Cause (Column 2)	Affects Our: (Column 3)
Person, Place or Thing		☐ Self-Esteem ☐ Security ☐ Ambitions ☐ Personal Relations ☐ Sex Relations ☐ Pride/Shame ☐ Fear
Ask Ourselves: ** (AA 67.3) * (AA 62.2)	Putting out of our mind the wrong others had done, we resolutely looked for our own mistakes… We admitted our wrongs honestly…** **STEPS 4 and/or 10 - (Column 4)**	
Where had I been selfish, self-centred or self-seeking?**		
Where had I been dishonest?**		
Where had I been frightened?**		
For what had I been responsible?**		
What decisions did I make based on self that later placed me in a position to be hurt?*		
When in the past did I make this decision? * (Earliest memory)		
Where was I wrong,** what was my part?		

STEPS 6 & 7 – List of Character Defects			

STEP 9 - Amends	STEP 8
	☐ Now ☐ Later ☐ Never

FORMS ONLY

INVENTORY FORMS

Resentment (1) and/or Fear:	The Cause (Column 2)	Affects Our: (Column 3)
Person, Place or Thing		☐ Self-Esteem ☐ Security ☐ Ambitions ☐ Personal Relations ☐ Sex Relations ☐ Pride/Shame ☐ Fear
Ask Ourselves: ** (AA 67.3) * (AA 62.2)	Putting out of our mind the wrong others had done, we resolutely looked for our own mistakes... We admitted our wrongs honestly...** **STEPS 4 and/or 10 - (Column 4)**	
Where had I been selfish, self-centred or self-seeking?**		
Where had I been dishonest?**		
Where had I been frightened?**		
For what had I been responsible?**		
What decisions did I make based on self that later placed me in a position to be hurt?*		
When in the past did I make this decision? * (Earliest memory)		
Where was I wrong,** what was my part?		

STEPS 6 & 7 – List of Character Defects			

STEP 9 - Amends		STEP 8
		☐ Now ☐ Later ☐ Never

144   FOUR COLUMN INVENTORY...

COLUMN WORK

Resentment (1) and/or Fear:	The Cause (Column 2)	Affects Our: (Column 3)
Person, Place or Thing		☐ Self-Esteem ☐ Security ☐ Ambitions ☐ Personal Relations ☐ Sex Relations ☐ Pride/Shame ☐ Fear
Ask Ourselves: ** (AA 67.3) * (AA 62.2)	Putting out of our mind the wrong others had done, we resolutely looked for our own mistakes... We admitted our wrongs honestly... ** **STEPS 4** and/or **10 - (Column 4)**	
Where had I been selfish, self-centred or self-seeking?**		
Where had I been dishonest?**		
Where had I been frightened?**		
For what had I been responsible?**		
What decisions did I make based on self that later placed me in a position to be hurt?*		
When in the past did I make this decision? * (Earliest memory)		
Where was I wrong,** what was my part?		

STEPS 6 & 7 – List of Character Defects

STEP 9 - Amends	STEP 8
	☐ Now ☐ Later ☐ Never

FORMS ONLY

INVENTORY FORMS

Resentment (1) and/or Fear:	The Cause (Column 2)	Affects Our: (Column 3)
Person, Place or Thing		☐ Self-Esteem ☐ Security ☐ Ambitions ☐ Personal Relations ☐ Sex Relations ☐ Pride/Shame ☐ Fear
Ask Ourselves: ** (AA 67.3) * (AA 62.2)	Putting out of our mind the wrong others had done, we resolutely looked for our own mistakes… We admitted our wrongs honestly…** **STEPS 4** and/or **10 - (Column 4)**	
Where had I been selfish, self-centred or self-seeking?**		
Where had I been dishonest?**		
Where had I been frightened?**		
For what had I been responsible?**		
What decisions did I make based on self that later placed me in a position to be hurt?*		
When in the past did I make this decision? * (Earliest memory)		
Where was I wrong,** what was my part?		

STEPS 6 & 7 – List of Character Defects			

STEP 9 - Amends	STEP 8
	☐ Now ☐ Later ☐ Never

FOUR COLUMN INVENTORY…

COLUMN WORK

Resentment (1) and/or Fear:	The Cause (Column 2)	Affects Our: (Column 3)
Person, Place or Thing		☐ Self-Esteem ☐ Security ☐ Ambitions ☐ Personal Relations ☐ Sex Relations ☐ Pride/Shame ☐ Fear

Ask Ourselves: ** (AA 67.3) * (AA 62.2)	Putting out of our mind the wrong others had done, we resolutely looked for our own mistakes… We admitted our wrongs honestly…** STEPS 4 and/or 10 - (Column 4)
Where had I been selfish, self-centred or self-seeking?**	
Where had I been dishonest?**	
Where had I been frightened?**	
For what had I been responsible?**	
What decisions did I make based on self that later placed me in a position to be hurt?*	
When in the past did I make this decision? * (Earliest memory)	
Where was I wrong,** what was my part?	

STEPS 6 & 7 – List of Character Defects

STEP 9 - Amends	STEP 8
	☐ Now ☐ Later ☐ Never

FORMS ONLY

INVENTORY FORMS

Resentment (1) and/or Fear:	The Cause (Column 2)	Affects Our: (Column 3)
Person, Place or Thing		☐ Self-Esteem ☐ Security ☐ Ambitions ☐ Personal Relations ☐ Sex Relations ☐ Pride/Shame ☐ Fear
Ask Ourselves: ** (AA 67.3) * (AA 62.2)	Putting out of our mind the wrong others had done, we resolutely looked for our own mistakes... We admitted our wrongs honestly...** **STEPS 4** and/or **10 - (Column 4)**	
Where had I been selfish, self-centred or self-seeking?**		
Where had I been dishonest?**		
Where had I been frightened?**		
For what had I been responsible?**		
What decisions did I make based on self that later placed me in a position to be hurt?*		
When in the past did I make this decision? * (Earliest memory)		
Where was I wrong,** what was my part?		

STEPS 6 & 7 – List of Character Defects			

STEP 9 - Amends	STEP 8
	☐ Now ☐ Later ☐ Never

COLUMN WORK

Resentment (1) and/or Fear:	The Cause (Column 2)	Affects Our: (Column 3)
Person, Place or Thing		☐ Self-Esteem ☐ Security ☐ Ambitions ☐ Personal Relations ☐ Sex Relations ☐ Pride/Shame ☐ Fear
Ask Ourselves: ** (AA 67.3) * (AA 62.2)	Putting out of our mind the wrong others had done, we resolutely looked for our own mistakes... We admitted our wrongs honestly...** **STEPS 4 and/or 10 - (Column 4)**	
Where had I been selfish, self-centred or self-seeking?**		
Where had I been dishonest?**		
Where had I been frightened?**		
For what had I been responsible?**		
What decisions did I make based on self that later placed me in a position to be hurt?*		
When in the past did I make this decision? * (Earliest memory)		
Where was I wrong,** what was my part?		

STEPS 6 & 7 – List of Character Defects			

STEP 9 - Amends	STEP 8
	☐ Now ☐ Later ☐ Never

FORMS ONLY

INVENTORY FORMS

Resentment (1) and/or Fear:	The Cause (Column 2)	Affects Our: (Column 3)
Person, Place or Thing		☐ Self-Esteem ☐ Security ☐ Ambitions ☐ Personal Relations ☐ Sex Relations ☐ Pride/Shame ☐ Fear
Ask Ourselves: ** (AA 67.3) * (AA 62.2)	Putting out of our mind the wrong others had done, we resolutely looked for our own mistakes… We admitted our wrongs honestly…** **STEPS 4 and/or 10 - (Column 4)**	
Where had I been selfish, self-centred or self-seeking?**		
Where had I been dishonest?**		
Where had I been frightened?**		
For what had I been responsible?**		
What decisions did I make based on self that later placed me in a position to be hurt?*		
When in the past did I make this decision? * (Earliest memory)		
Where was I wrong,** what was my part?		

STEPS 6 & 7 – List of Character Defects

STEP 9 - Amends	STEP 8
	☐ Now ☐ Later ☐ Never

COLUMN WORK

Resentment (1) and/or Fear:	The Cause (Column 2)	Affects Our: (Column 3)
Person, Place or Thing		☐ Self-Esteem ☐ Security ☐ Ambitions ☐ Personal Relations ☐ Sex Relations ☐ Pride/Shame ☐ Fear
Ask Ourselves: ** (AA 67.3) * (AA 62.2)	Putting out of our mind the wrong others had done, we resolutely looked for our own mistakes... We admitted our wrongs honestly...** **STEPS 4** and/or **10 - (Column 4)**	
Where had I been selfish, self-centred or self-seeking?**		
Where had I been dishonest?**		
Where had I been frightened?**		
For what had I been responsible?**		
What decisions did I make based on self that later placed me in a position to be hurt?*		
When in the past did I make this decision? * (Earliest memory)		
Where was I wrong,** what was my part?		

STEPS 6 & 7 – List of Character Defects

STEP 9 - Amends	STEP 8
	☐ Now ☐ Later ☐ Never

FORMS ONLY

INVENTORY FORMS

Resentment (1) and/or Fear:	The Cause (Column 2)	Affects Our: (Column 3)
Person, Place or Thing		☐ Self-Esteem ☐ Security ☐ Ambitions ☐ Personal Relations ☐ Sex Relations ☐ Pride/Shame ☐ Fear
Ask Ourselves: ** (AA 67.3) * (AA 62.2)	Putting out of our mind the wrong others had done, we resolutely looked for our own mistakes... We admitted our wrongs honestly...** **STEPS 4** and/or **10** - **(Column 4)**	
Where had I been selfish, self-centred or self-seeking?**		
Where had I been dishonest?**		
Where had I been frightened?**		
For what had I been responsible?**		
What decisions did I make based on self that later placed me in a position to be hurt?*		
When in the past did I make this decision? * (Earliest memory)		
Where was I wrong,** what was my part?		
STEPS 6 & 7 – List of Character Defects		
STEP 9 - Amends		**STEP 8**
		☐ Now ☐ Later ☐ Never

COLUMN WORK

Resentment (1) and/or Fear:	The Cause (Column 2)	Affects Our: (Column 3)
Person, Place or Thing		☐ Self-Esteem ☐ Security ☐ Ambitions ☐ Personal Relations ☐ Sex Relations ☐ Pride/Shame ☐ Fear
Ask Ourselves: ** (AA 67.3) * (AA 62.2)	Putting out of our mind the wrong others had done, we resolutely looked for our own mistakes… We admitted our wrongs honestly…** **STEPS 4 and/or 10 - (Column 4)**	
Where had I been selfish, self-centred or self-seeking?**		
Where had I been dishonest?**		
Where had I been frightened?**		
For what had I been responsible?**		
What decisions did I make based on self that later placed me in a position to be hurt?*		
When in the past did I make this decision? * (Earliest memory)		
Where was I wrong,** what was my part?		

STEPS 6 & 7 – List of Character Defects

STEP 9 - Amends	STEP 8
	☐ Now ☐ Later ☐ Never

INVENTORY FORMS

Resentment (1) and/or Fear:	The Cause (Column 2)	Affects Our: (Column 3)
Person, Place or Thing		☐ Self-Esteem ☐ Security ☐ Ambitions ☐ Personal Relations ☐ Sex Relations ☐ Pride/Shame ☐ Fear
Ask Ourselves: ** (AA 67.3) * (AA 62.2)	Putting out of our mind the wrong others had done, we resolutely looked for our own mistakes... We admitted our wrongs honestly...** **STEPS 4** and/or **10** - **(Column 4)**	
Where had I been selfish, self-centred or self-seeking?**		
Where had I been dishonest?**		
Where had I been frightened?**		
For what had I been responsible?**		
What decisions did I make based on self that later placed me in a position to be hurt?*		
When in the past did I make this decision? * (Earliest memory)		
Where was I wrong,** what was my part?		

STEPS 6 & 7 – List of Character Defects			

STEP 9 - Amends	STEP 8
	☐ **Now** ☐ **Later** ☐ **Never**

154   FOUR COLUMN INVENTORY...

COLUMN WORK

Resentment (1) and/or Fear:	The Cause (Column 2)	Affects Our: (Column 3)
Person, Place or Thing		☐ Self-Esteem ☐ Security ☐ Ambitions ☐ Personal Relations ☐ Sex Relations ☐ Pride/Shame ☐ Fear
Ask Ourselves: ** (AA 67.3) * (AA 62.2)	Putting out of our mind the wrong others had done, we resolutely looked for our own mistakes... We admitted our wrongs honestly...** **STEPS 4 and/or 10 - (Column 4)**	
Where had I been selfish, self-centred or self-seeking?**		
Where had I been dishonest?**		
Where had I been frightened?**		
For what had I been responsible?**		
What decisions did I make based on self that later placed me in a position to be hurt?*		
When in the past did I make this decision? * (Earliest memory)		
Where was I wrong,** what was my part?		

STEPS 6 & 7 – List of Character Defects				

STEP 9 - Amends	STEP 8
	☐ Now ☐ Later ☐ Never

FORMS ONLY

INVENTORY FORMS

Resentment (1) and/or Fear:	The Cause (Column 2)	Affects Our: (Column 3)
Person, Place or Thing		☐ Self-Esteem ☐ Security ☐ Ambitions ☐ Personal Relations ☐ Sex Relations ☐ Pride/Shame ☐ Fear
Ask Ourselves: ** (AA 67.3) * (AA 62.2)	Putting out of our mind the wrong others had done, we resolutely looked for our own mistakes... We admitted our wrongs honestly...** **STEPS 4** and/or **10 - (Column 4)**	
Where had I been selfish, self-centred or self-seeking?**		
Where had I been dishonest?**		
Where had I been frightened?**		
For what had I been responsible?**		
What decisions did I make based on self that later placed me in a position to be hurt?*		
When in the past did I make this decision? * (Earliest memory)		
Where was I wrong,** what was my part?		

STEPS 6 & 7 – List of Character Defects

STEP 9 - Amends	STEP 8
	☐ Now ☐ Later ☐ Never

FOUR COLUMN INVENTORY...

COLUMN WORK

Resentment (1) and/or Fear:	The Cause (Column 2)	Affects Our: (Column 3)
Person, Place or Thing		☐ Self-Esteem ☐ Security ☐ Ambitions ☐ Personal Relations ☐ Sex Relations ☐ Pride/Shame ☐ Fear
Ask Ourselves: ** (AA 67.3) * (AA 62.2)	Putting out of our mind the wrong others had done, we resolutely looked for our own mistakes... We admitted our wrongs honestly...** **STEPS 4 and/or 10 - (Column 4)**	
Where had I been selfish, self-centred or self-seeking?**		
Where had I been dishonest?**		
Where had I been frightened?**		
For what had I been responsible?**		
What decisions did I make based on self that later placed me in a position to be hurt?*		
When in the past did I make this decision? * (Earliest memory)		
Where was I wrong,** what was my part?		

STEPS 6 & 7 – List of Character Defects				

STEP 9 - Amends	STEP 8
	☐ Now ☐ Later ☐ Never

FORMS ONLY

INVENTORY FORMS

Resentment (1) and/or Fear:	The Cause (Column 2)	Affects Our: (Column 3)
Person, Place or Thing		☐ Self-Esteem ☐ Security ☐ Ambitions ☐ Personal Relations ☐ Sex Relations ☐ Pride/Shame ☐ Fear
Ask Ourselves: ** (AA 67.3) * (AA 62.2)	Putting out of our mind the wrong others had done, we resolutely looked for our own mistakes… We admitted our wrongs honestly…** **STEPS 4** and/or **10** - **(Column 4)**	
Where had I been selfish, self-centred or self-seeking?**		
Where had I been dishonest?**		
Where had I been frightened?**		
For what had I been responsible?**		
What decisions did I make based on self that later placed me in a position to be hurt?*		
When in the past did I make this decision? * (Earliest memory)		
Where was I wrong,** what was my part?		

STEPS 6 & 7 – List of Character Defects				

STEP 9 - Amends	STEP 8
	☐ Now ☐ Later ☐ Never

COLUMN WORK

Resentment (1) and/or Fear:	The Cause (Column 2)	Affects Our: (Column 3)
Person, Place or Thing		☐ Self-Esteem ☐ Security ☐ Ambitions ☐ Personal Relations ☐ Sex Relations ☐ Pride/Shame ☐ Fear
Ask Ourselves: ** (AA 67.3) * (AA 62.2)	Putting out of our mind the wrong others had done, we resolutely looked for our own mistakes... We admitted our wrongs honestly... ** **STEPS 4 and/or 10 - (Column 4)**	
Where had I been selfish, self-centred or self-seeking?**		
Where had I been dishonest?**		
Where had I been frightened?**		
For what had I been responsible?**		
What decisions did I make based on self that later placed me in a position to be hurt?*		
When in the past did I make this decision? * (Earliest memory)		
Where was I wrong,** what was my part?		

STEPS 6 & 7 – List of Character Defects

STEP 9 - Amends	STEP 8
	☐ Now ☐ Later ☐ Never

FORMS ONLY

INVENTORY FORMS

Resentment (1) and/or Fear:	The Cause (Column 2)	Affects Our: (Column 3)
Person, Place or Thing		☐ Self-Esteem ☐ Security ☐ Ambitions ☐ Personal Relations ☐ Sex Relations ☐ Pride/Shame ☐ Fear
Ask Ourselves: ** (AA 67.3) * (AA 62.2)	Putting out of our mind the wrong others had done, we resolutely looked for our own mistakes... We admitted our wrongs honestly...** **STEPS 4** and/or **10 - (Column 4)**	
Where had I been selfish, self-centred or self-seeking?**		
Where had I been dishonest?**		
Where had I been frightened?**		
For what had I been responsible?**		
What decisions did I make based on self that later placed me in a position to be hurt?*		
When in the past did I make this decision? * (Earliest memory)		
Where was I wrong,** what was my part?		

STEPS 6 & 7 – List of Character Defects			

STEP 9 - Amends	STEP 8
	☐ Now ☐ Later ☐ Never

FOUR COLUMN INVENTORY...

COLUMN WORK

Resentment (1) and/or Fear:	The Cause (Column 2)	Affects Our: (Column 3)
Person, Place or Thing		☐ Self-Esteem ☐ Security ☐ Ambitions ☐ Personal Relations ☐ Sex Relations ☐ Pride/Shame ☐ Fear
Ask Ourselves: ** (AA 67.3) * (AA 62.2)	Putting out of our mind the wrong others had done, we resolutely looked for our own mistakes... We admitted our wrongs honestly...** **STEPS 4 and/or 10 - (Column 4)**	
Where had I been selfish, self-centred or self-seeking?**		
Where had I been dishonest?**		
Where had I been frightened?**		
For what had I been responsible?**		
What decisions did I make based on self that later placed me in a position to be hurt?*		
When in the past did I make this decision? * (Earliest memory)		
Where was I wrong,** what was my part?		
STEPS 6 & 7 – List of Character Defects					
STEP 9 - Amends			**STEP 8**
			☐ Now ☐ Later ☐ Never

FORMS ONLY

INVENTORY FORMS

Resentment (1) and/or Fear:	The Cause (Column 2)	Affects Our: (Column 3)
Person, Place or Thing		☐ Self-Esteem ☐ Security ☐ Ambitions ☐ Personal Relations ☐ Sex Relations ☐ Pride/Shame ☐ Fear
Ask Ourselves: ** (AA 67.3) * (AA 62.2)	Putting out of our mind the wrong others had done, we resolutely looked for our own mistakes... We admitted our wrongs honestly...** **STEPS 4** and/or **10 - (Column 4)**	
Where had I been selfish, self-centred or self-seeking?**		
Where had I been dishonest?**		
Where had I been frightened?**		
For what had I been responsible?**		
What decisions did I make based on self that later placed me in a position to be hurt?*		
When in the past did I make this decision? * (Earliest memory)		
Where was I wrong,** what was my part?		
STEPS 6 & 7 – List of Character Defects			
STEP 9 - Amends			**STEP 8**
			☐ **Now** ☐ **Later** ☐ **Never**

162   FOUR COLUMN INVENTORY...

COLUMN WORK

Resentment (1) and/or Fear:	The Cause (Column 2)	Affects Our: (Column 3)
Person, Place or Thing		☐ Self-Esteem ☐ Security ☐ Ambitions ☐ Personal Relations ☐ Sex Relations ☐ Pride/Shame ☐ Fear
Ask Ourselves: ** (AA 67.3) * (AA 62.2)	Putting out of our mind the wrong others had done, we resolutely looked for our own mistakes… We admitted our wrongs honestly…** **STEPS 4 and/or 10 - (Column 4)**	
Where had I been selfish, self-centred or self-seeking?**		
Where had I been dishonest?**		
Where had I been frightened?**		
For what had I been responsible?**		
What decisions did I make based on self that later placed me in a position to be hurt?*		
When in the past did I make this decision? * (Earliest memory)		
Where was I wrong,** what was my part?		

STEPS 6 & 7 – List of Character Defects

STEP 9 - Amends	STEP 8
	☐ Now ☐ Later ☐ Never

INVENTORY FORMS

Resentment (1) and/or Fear:	The Cause (Column 2)	Affects Our: (Column 3)
Person, Place or Thing		☐ Self-Esteem ☐ Security ☐ Ambitions ☐ Personal Relations ☐ Sex Relations ☐ Pride/Shame ☐ Fear
Ask Ourselves: ** (AA 67.3) * (AA 62.2)	Putting out of our mind the wrong others had done, we resolutely looked for our own mistakes... We admitted our wrongs honestly...** **STEPS 4 and/or 10 - (Column 4)**	
Where had I been selfish, self-centred or self-seeking?**		
Where had I been dishonest?**		
Where had I been frightened?**		
For what had I been responsible?**		
What decisions did I make based on self that later placed me in a position to be hurt?*		
When in the past did I make this decision? * (Earliest memory)		
Where was I wrong,** what was my part?		

STEPS 6 & 7 – List of Character Defects

STEP 9 - Amends	STEP 8
	☐ Now ☐ Later ☐ Never

COLUMN WORK

Resentment (1) and/or Fear:	The Cause (Column 2)	Affects Our: (Column 3)
Person, Place or Thing		☐ Self-Esteem ☐ Security ☐ Ambitions ☐ Personal Relations ☐ Sex Relations ☐ Pride/Shame ☐ Fear
Ask Ourselves: ** (AA 67.3) * (AA 62.2)	Putting out of our mind the wrong others had done, we resolutely looked for our own mistakes... We admitted our wrongs honestly... ** **STEPS 4 and/or 10 - (Column 4)**	
Where had I been selfish, self-centred or self-seeking?**		
Where had I been dishonest?**		
Where had I been frightened?**		
For what had I been responsible?**		
What decisions did I make based on self that later placed me in a position to be hurt?*		
When in the past did I make this decision? * (Earliest memory)		
Where was I wrong,** what was my part?		
STEPS 6 & 7 – List of Character Defects		
STEP 9 - Amends		**STEP 8**
		☐ Now ☐ Later ☐ Never

INVENTORY FORMS

Resentment (1) and/or Fear:	The Cause (Column 2)	Affects Our: (Column 3)
Person, Place or Thing		☐ Self-Esteem ☐ Security ☐ Ambitions ☐ Personal Relations ☐ Sex Relations ☐ Pride/Shame ☐ Fear
Ask Ourselves: ** (AA 67.3) * (AA 62.2)	Putting out of our mind the wrong others had done, we resolutely looked for our own mistakes… We admitted our wrongs honestly…** **STEPS 4** and/or **10** - **(Column 4)**	
Where had I been selfish, self-centred or self-seeking?**		
Where had I been dishonest?**		
Where had I been frightened?**		
For what had I been responsible?**		
What decisions did I make based on self that later placed me in a position to be hurt?*		
When in the past did I make this decision? * (Earliest memory)		
Where was I wrong,** what was my part?		

STEPS 6 & 7 – List of Character Defects			

STEP 9 - Amends	STEP 8
	☐ **Now** ☐ **Later** ☐ **Never**

166   FOUR COLUMN INVENTORY…

COLUMN WORK

Resentment (1) and/or Fear:	The Cause (Column 2)	Affects Our: (Column 3)
Person, Place or Thing		☐ Self-Esteem ☐ Security ☐ Ambitions ☐ Personal Relations ☐ Sex Relations ☐ Pride/Shame ☐ Fear
Ask Ourselves: ** (AA 67.3) * (AA 62.2)	Putting out of our mind the wrong others had done, we resolutely looked for our own mistakes... We admitted our wrongs honestly...** **STEPS 4 and/or 10 - (Column 4)**	
Where had I been selfish, self-centred or self-seeking?**		
Where had I been dishonest?**		
Where had I been frightened?**		
For what had I been responsible?**		
What decisions did I make based on self that later placed me in a position to be hurt?*		
When in the past did I make this decision? * (Earliest memory)		
Where was I wrong,** what was my part?		

STEPS 6 & 7 – List of Character Defects			

STEP 9 - Amends	STEP 8
	☐ Now ☐ Later ☐ Never

FORMS ONLY

INVENTORY FORMS

Resentment (1) and/or Fear:	The Cause (Column 2)	Affects Our: (Column 3)
Person, Place or Thing		☐ Self-Esteem ☐ Security ☐ Ambitions ☐ Personal Relations ☐ Sex Relations ☐ Pride/Shame ☐ Fear
Ask Ourselves: ** (AA 67.3) * (AA 62.2)	Putting out of our mind the wrong others had done, we resolutely looked for our own mistakes... We admitted our wrongs honestly...** **STEPS 4** and/or **10** - **(Column 4)**	
Where had I been selfish, self-centred or self-seeking?**		
Where had I been dishonest?**		
Where had I been frightened?**		
For what had I been responsible?**		
What decisions did I make based on self that later placed me in a position to be hurt?*		
When in the past did I make this decision? * (Earliest memory)		
Where was I wrong,** what was my part?		
STEPS 6 & 7 – List of Character Defects			
STEP 9 - Amends	**STEP 8**
	☐ **Now** ☐ **Later** ☐ **Never**

COLUMN WORK

Resentment (1) and/or Fear:	The Cause (Column 2)	Affects Our: (Column 3)
Person, Place or Thing		☐ Self-Esteem ☐ Security ☐ Ambitions ☐ Personal Relations ☐ Sex Relations ☐ Pride/Shame ☐ Fear
Ask Ourselves: ** (AA 67.3) * (AA 62.2)	Putting out of our mind the wrong others had done, we resolutely looked for our own mistakes... We admitted our wrongs honestly...** **STEPS 4 and/or 10 - (Column 4)**	
Where had I been selfish, self-centred or self-seeking?**		
Where had I been dishonest?**		
Where had I been frightened?**		
For what had I been responsible?**		
What decisions did I make based on self that later placed me in a position to be hurt?*		
When in the past did I make this decision? * (Earliest memory)		
Where was I wrong,** what was my part?		

STEPS 6 & 7 – List of Character Defects

STEP 9 - Amends | STEP 8

☐ Now
☐ Later
☐ Never

FORMS ONLY

INVENTORY FORMS

Resentment (1) and/or Fear:	The Cause (Column 2)	Affects Our: (Column 3)
Person, Place or Thing		☐ Self-Esteem ☐ Security ☐ Ambitions ☐ Personal Relations ☐ Sex Relations ☐ Pride/Shame ☐ Fear
Ask Ourselves: ** (AA 67.3) * (AA 62.2)	Putting out of our mind the wrong others had done, we resolutely looked for our own mistakes... We admitted our wrongs honestly...** **STEPS 4 and/or 10 - (Column 4)**	
Where had I been selfish, self-centred or self-seeking?**		
Where had I been dishonest?**		
Where had I been frightened?**		
For what had I been responsible?**		
What decisions did I make based on self that later placed me in a position to be hurt?*		
When in the past did I make this decision? * (Earliest memory)		
Where was I wrong,** what was my part?		

STEPS 6 & 7 – List of Character Defects			

STEP 9 - Amends	STEP 8
	☐ Now ☐ Later ☐ Never

170 FOUR COLUMN INVENTORY...

COLUMN WORK

Resentment (1) and/or Fear:	The Cause (Column 2)	Affects Our: (Column 3)
Person, Place or Thing		☐ Self-Esteem ☐ Security ☐ Ambitions ☐ Personal Relations ☐ Sex Relations ☐ Pride/Shame ☐ Fear
Ask Ourselves: ** (AA 67.3) * (AA 62.2)	Putting out of our mind the wrong others had done, we resolutely looked for our own mistakes… We admitted our wrongs honestly…** **STEPS 4 and/or 10 - (Column 4)**	
Where had I been selfish, self-centred or self-seeking?**		
Where had I been dishonest?**		
Where had I been frightened?**		
For what had I been responsible?**		
What decisions did I make based on self that later placed me in a position to be hurt?*		
When in the past did I make this decision? * (Earliest memory)		
Where was I wrong,** what was my part?		

STEPS 6 & 7 – List of Character Defects				

STEP 9 - Amends	STEP 8
	☐ Now ☐ Later ☐ Never

INVENTORY FORMS

Resentment (1) and/or Fear:	The Cause (Column 2)	Affects Our: (Column 3)
Person, Place or Thing		☐ Self-Esteem ☐ Security ☐ Ambitions ☐ Personal Relations ☐ Sex Relations ☐ Pride/Shame ☐ Fear
Ask Ourselves: ** (AA 67.3) * (AA 62.2)	Putting out of our mind the wrong others had done, we resolutely looked for our own mistakes… We admitted our wrongs honestly…** **STEPS 4** and/or **10 - (Column 4)**	
Where had I been selfish, self-centred or self-seeking?**		
Where had I been dishonest?**		
Where had I been frightened?**		
For what had I been responsible?**		
What decisions did I make based on self that later placed me in a position to be hurt?*		
When in the past did I make this decision? * (Earliest memory)		
Where was I wrong,** what was my part?		

STEPS 6 & 7 – List of Character Defects			

STEP 9 - Amends	STEP 8
	☐ **Now** ☐ **Later** ☐ **Never**

COLUMN WORK

Resentment (1) and/or Fear:	The Cause (Column 2)	Affects Our: (Column 3)
Person, Place or Thing		☐ Self-Esteem ☐ Security ☐ Ambitions ☐ Personal Relations ☐ Sex Relations ☐ Pride/Shame ☐ Fear
Ask Ourselves: ** (AA 67.3) * (AA 62.2)	Putting out of our mind the wrong others had done, we resolutely looked for our own mistakes... We admitted our wrongs honestly...** **STEPS 4** and/or **10 - (Column 4)**	
Where had I been selfish, self-centred or self-seeking?**		
Where had I been dishonest?**		
Where had I been frightened?**		
For what had I been responsible?**		
What decisions did I make based on self that later placed me in a position to be hurt?*		
When in the past did I make this decision? * (Earliest memory)		
Where was I wrong,** what was my part?		

STEPS 6 & 7 – List of Character Defects

STEP 9 - Amends	STEP 8
	☐ Now ☐ Later ☐ Never

FORMS ONLY

INVENTORY FORMS

Resentment (1) and/or Fear:	The Cause (Column 2)	Affects Our: (Column 3)
Person, Place or Thing		☐ Self-Esteem ☐ Security ☐ Ambitions ☐ Personal Relations ☐ Sex Relations ☐ Pride/Shame ☐ Fear
Ask Ourselves: ** (AA 67.3) * (AA 62.2)	Putting out of our mind the wrong others had done, we resolutely looked for our own mistakes... We admitted our wrongs honestly...** **STEPS 4 and/or 10 - (Column 4)**	
Where had I been selfish, self-centred or self-seeking?**		
Where had I been dishonest?**		
Where had I been frightened?**		
For what had I been responsible?**		
What decisions did I make based on self that later placed me in a position to be hurt?*		
When in the past did I make this decision? * (Earliest memory)		
Where was I wrong,** what was my part?		

STEPS 6 & 7 – List of Character Defects				

STEP 9 - Amends	STEP 8
	☐ Now ☐ Later ☐ Never

FOUR COLUMN INVENTORY...

COLUMN WORK

Resentment (1) and/or Fear:	The Cause (Column 2)	Affects Our: (Column 3)
Person, Place or Thing		☐ Self-Esteem ☐ Security ☐ Ambitions ☐ Personal Relations ☐ Sex Relations ☐ Pride/Shame ☐ Fear
Ask Ourselves: ** (AA 67.3) * (AA 62.2)	Putting out of our mind the wrong others had done, we resolutely looked for our own mistakes… We admitted our wrongs honestly…** STEPS 4 and/or **10 - (Column 4)**	
Where had I been selfish, self-centred or self-seeking?**		
Where had I been dishonest?**		
Where had I been frightened?**		
For what had I been responsible?**		
What decisions did I make based on self that later placed me in a position to be hurt?*		
When in the past did I make this decision? * (Earliest memory)		
Where was I wrong,** what was my part?		

STEPS 6 & 7 – List of Character Defects

STEP 9 - Amends	STEP 8
	☐ Now ☐ Later ☐ Never

FORMS ONLY

INVENTORY FORMS

Resentment (1) and/or Fear:	The Cause (Column 2)	Affects Our: (Column 3)
Person, Place or Thing		☐ Self-Esteem ☐ Security ☐ Ambitions ☐ Personal Relations ☐ Sex Relations ☐ Pride/Shame ☐ Fear
Ask Ourselves: ** (AA 67.3) * (AA 62.2)	Putting out of our mind the wrong others had done, we resolutely looked for our own mistakes... We admitted our wrongs honestly...** **STEPS 4** and/or **10 - (Column 4)**	
Where had I been selfish, self-centred or self-seeking?**		
Where had I been dishonest?**		
Where had I been frightened?**		
For what had I been responsible?**		
What decisions did I make based on self that later placed me in a position to be hurt?*		
When in the past did I make this decision? * (Earliest memory)		
Where was I wrong,** what was my part?		

STEPS 6 & 7 – List of Character Defects

STEP 9 - Amends	STEP 8
	☐ **Now** ☐ **Later** ☐ **Never**

176   FOUR COLUMN INVENTORY...

COLUMN WORK

Resentment (1) and/or Fear:	The Cause (Column 2)	Affects Our: (Column 3)
Person, Place or Thing		☐ Self-Esteem ☐ Security ☐ Ambitions ☐ Personal Relations ☐ Sex Relations ☐ Pride/Shame ☐ Fear
Ask Ourselves: ** (AA 67.3) * (AA 62.2)	Putting out of our mind the wrong others had done, we resolutely looked for our own mistakes… We admitted our wrongs honestly…** **STEPS 4** and/or **10** - **(Column 4)**	
Where had I been selfish, self-centred or self-seeking?**		
Where had I been dishonest?**		
Where had I been frightened?**		
For what had I been responsible?**		
What decisions did I make based on self that later placed me in a position to be hurt?*		
When in the past did I make this decision? * (Earliest memory)		
Where was I wrong,** what was my part?		

STEPS 6 & 7 – List of Character Defects			

STEP 9 - Amends	STEP 8
	☐ Now ☐ Later ☐ Never

INVENTORY FORMS

Resentment and/or Fear: (1)	The Cause (Column 2)	Affects Our: (Column 3)
Person, Place or Thing		☐ Self-Esteem ☐ Security ☐ Ambitions ☐ Personal Relations ☐ Sex Relations ☐ Pride/Shame ☐ Fear
Ask Ourselves: ** (AA 67.3) * (AA 62.2)	Putting out of our mind the wrong others had done, we resolutely looked for our own mistakes... We admitted our wrongs honestly...** **STEPS 4** and/or **10 - (Column 4)**	
Where had I been selfish, self-centred or self-seeking?**		
Where had I been dishonest?**		
Where had I been frightened?**		
For what had I been responsible?**		
What decisions did I make based on self that later placed me in a position to be hurt?*		
When in the past did I make this decision? * (Earliest memory)		
Where was I wrong,** what was my part?		
STEPS 6 & 7 – List of Character Defects			
STEP 9 - Amends		**STEP 8**
		☐ Now ☐ Later ☐ Never

FOUR COLUMN INVENTORY...

COLUMN WORK

Resentment (1) and/or Fear:	The Cause (Column 2)	Affects Our: (Column 3)
Person, Place or Thing		☐ Self-Esteem ☐ Security ☐ Ambitions ☐ Personal Relations ☐ Sex Relations ☐ Pride/Shame ☐ Fear
Ask Ourselves: ** (AA 67.3) * (AA 62.2)	Putting out of our mind the wrong others had done, we resolutely looked for our own mistakes... We admitted our wrongs honestly...** STEPS 4 and/or 10 - (Column 4)	
Where had I been selfish, self-centred or self-seeking?**		
Where had I been dishonest?**		
Where had I been frightened?**		
For what had I been responsible?**		
What decisions did I make based on self that later placed me in a position to be hurt?*		
When in the past did I make this decision? * (Earliest memory)		
Where was I wrong,** what was my part?		

STEPS 6 & 7 – List of Character Defects				

STEP 9 - Amends	STEP 8
	☐ Now ☐ Later ☐ Never

FORMS ONLY

INVENTORY FORMS

Resentment (1) and/or Fear:	The Cause (Column 2)	Affects Our: (Column 3)
Person, Place or Thing		☐ Self-Esteem ☐ Security ☐ Ambitions ☐ Personal Relations ☐ Sex Relations ☐ Pride/Shame ☐ Fear
Ask Ourselves: ** (AA 67.3) * (AA 62.2)	Putting out of our mind the wrong others had done, we resolutely looked for our own mistakes... We admitted our wrongs honestly...** **STEPS 4** and/or **10 - (Column 4)**	
Where had I been selfish, self-centred or self-seeking?**		
Where had I been dishonest?**		
Where had I been frightened?**		
For what had I been responsible?**		
What decisions did I make based on self that later placed me in a position to be hurt?*		
When in the past did I make this decision? * (Earliest memory)		
Where was I wrong,** what was my part?		
STEPS 6 & 7 – List of Character Defects		
STEP 9 - Amends		**STEP 8** ☐ **Now** ☐ **Later** ☐ **Never**

FOUR COLUMN INVENTORY...

COLUMN WORK

Resentment (1) and/or Fear:	The Cause (Column 2)	Affects Our: (Column 3)
Person, Place or Thing		☐ Self-Esteem ☐ Security ☐ Ambitions ☐ Personal Relations ☐ Sex Relations ☐ Pride/Shame ☐ Fear
Ask Ourselves: ** (AA 67.3) * (AA 62.2)	Putting out of our mind the wrong others had done, we resolutely looked for our own mistakes… We admitted our wrongs honestly…** **STEPS 4** and/or **10** - **(Column 4)**	
Where had I been selfish, self-centred or self-seeking?**		
Where had I been dishonest?**		
Where had I been frightened?**		
For what had I been responsible?**		
What decisions did I make based on self that later placed me in a position to be hurt?*		
When in the past did I make this decision? * (Earliest memory)		
Where was I wrong,** what was my part?		

STEPS 6 & 7 – List of Character Defects				

STEP 9 - Amends	STEP 8
	☐ Now ☐ Later ☐ Never

FORMS ONLY

INVENTORY FORMS

Resentment (1) and/or Fear:	The Cause (Column 2)	Affects Our: (Column 3)
Person, Place or Thing		☐ Self-Esteem ☐ Security ☐ Ambitions ☐ Personal Relations ☐ Sex Relations ☐ Pride/Shame ☐ Fear
Ask Ourselves: ** (AA 67.3) * (AA 62.2)	Putting out of our mind the wrong others had done, we resolutely looked for our own mistakes... We admitted our wrongs honestly...** **STEPS 4 and/or 10 - (Column 4)**	
Where had I been selfish, self-centred or self-seeking?**		
Where had I been dishonest?**		
Where had I been frightened?**		
For what had I been responsible?**		
What decisions did I make based on self that later placed me in a position to be hurt?*		
When in the past did I make this decision? * (Earliest memory)		
Where was I wrong,** what was my part?		

STEPS 6 & 7 – List of Character Defects			

STEP 9 - Amends	STEP 8
	☐ Now ☐ Later ☐ Never

COLUMN WORK

Resentment (1) and/or Fear:	The Cause (Column 2)	Affects Our: (Column 3)
Person, Place or Thing		☐ Self-Esteem ☐ Security ☐ Ambitions ☐ Personal Relations ☐ Sex Relations ☐ Pride/Shame ☐ Fear
Ask Ourselves: ** (AA 67.3) * (AA 62.2)	Putting out of our mind the wrong others had done, we resolutely looked for our own mistakes… We admitted our wrongs honestly… ** **STEPS 4** and/or **10 - (Column 4)**	
Where had I been selfish, self-centred or self-seeking?**		
Where had I been dishonest?**		
Where had I been frightened?**		
For what had I been responsible?**		
What decisions did I make based on self that later placed me in a position to be hurt?*		
When in the past did I make this decision? * (Earliest memory)		
Where was I wrong,** what was my part?		

STEPS 6 & 7 – List of Character Defects				

STEP 9 - Amends	STEP 8
	☐ Now ☐ Later ☐ Never

FORMS ONLY

INVENTORY FORMS

Resentment and/or Fear: (1)	The Cause (Column 2)	Affects Our: (Column 3)
Person, Place or Thing		☐ Self-Esteem ☐ Security ☐ Ambitions ☐ Personal Relations ☐ Sex Relations ☐ Pride/Shame ☐ Fear
Ask Ourselves: ** (AA 67.3) * (AA 62.2)	Putting out of our mind the wrong others had done, we resolutely looked for our own mistakes... We admitted our wrongs honestly...** **STEPS 4** and/or **10 - (Column 4)**	
Where had I been selfish, self-centred or self-seeking?**		
Where had I been dishonest?**		
Where had I been frightened?**		
For what had I been responsible?**		
What decisions did I make based on self that later placed me in a position to be hurt?*		
When in the past did I make this decision? * (Earliest memory)		
Where was I wrong,** what was my part?		

STEPS 6 & 7 – List of Character Defects				

STEP 9 - Amends	STEP 8
	☐ Now ☐ Later ☐ Never

COLUMN WORK

Resentment (1) and/or Fear:	The Cause (Column 2)	Affects Our: (Column 3)
Person, Place or Thing		☐ Self-Esteem ☐ Security ☐ Ambitions ☐ Personal Relations ☐ Sex Relations ☐ Pride/Shame ☐ Fear
Ask Ourselves: ** (AA 67.3) * (AA 62.2)	Putting out of our mind the wrong others had done, we resolutely looked for our own mistakes… We admitted our wrongs honestly…** **STEPS 4 and/or 10 - (Column 4)**	
Where had I been selfish, self-centred or self-seeking?**		
Where had I been dishonest?**		
Where had I been frightened?**		
For what had I been responsible?**		
What decisions did I make based on self that later placed me in a position to be hurt?*		
When in the past did I make this decision? * (Earliest memory)		
Where was I wrong,** what was my part?		

STEPS 6 & 7 – List of Character Defects			

STEP 9 - Amends	STEP 8
	☐ Now ☐ Later ☐ Never

FORMS ONLY

INVENTORY FORMS

Resentment (1) and/or Fear:	The Cause (Column 2)	Affects Our: (Column 3)
Person, Place or Thing		☐ Self-Esteem ☐ Security ☐ Ambitions ☐ Personal Relations ☐ Sex Relations ☐ Pride/Shame ☐ Fear
Ask Ourselves: ** (AA 67.3) * (AA 62.2)	Putting out of our mind the wrong others had done, we resolutely looked for our own mistakes… We admitted our wrongs honestly… ** **STEPS 4 and/or 10 - (Column 4)**	
Where had I been selfish, self-centred or self-seeking?**		
Where had I been dishonest?**		
Where had I been frightened?**		
For what had I been responsible?**		
What decisions did I make based on self that later placed me in a position to be hurt?*		
When in the past did I make this decision? * (Earliest memory)		
Where was I wrong,** what was my part?		
STEPS 6 & 7 – List of Character Defects			
STEP 9 - Amends		**STEP 8**
		☐ Now ☐ Later ☐ Never

COLUMN WORK

Resentment (1) and/or Fear:	The Cause (Column 2)	Affects Our: (Column 3)
Person, Place or Thing		☐ Self-Esteem ☐ Security ☐ Ambitions ☐ Personal Relations ☐ Sex Relations ☐ Pride/Shame ☐ Fear
Ask Ourselves: ** (AA 67.3) * (AA 62.2)	Putting out of our mind the wrong others had done, we resolutely looked for our own mistakes… We admitted our wrongs honestly…** **STEPS 4** and/or **10 - (Column 4)**	
Where had I been selfish, self-centred or self-seeking?**		
Where had I been dishonest?**		
Where had I been frightened?**		
For what had I been responsible?**		
What decisions did I make based on self that later placed me in a position to be hurt?*		
When in the past did I make this decision? * (Earliest memory)		
Where was I wrong,** what was my part?		

STEPS 6 & 7 – List of Character Defects

STEP 9 - Amends	STEP 8
	☐ Now ☐ Later ☐ Never

FORMS ONLY

INVENTORY FORMS

Resentment (1) and/or Fear:	The Cause (Column 2)	Affects Our: (Column 3)
Person, Place or Thing		❏ Self-Esteem ❏ Security ❏ Ambitions ❏ Personal Relations ❏ Sex Relations ❏ Pride/Shame ❏ Fear
Ask Ourselves: ** (AA 67.3) * (AA 62.2)	Putting out of our mind the wrong others had done, we resolutely looked for our own mistakes... We admitted our wrongs honestly...** **STEPS 4** and/or **10 - (Column 4)**	
Where had I been selfish, self-centred or self-seeking?**		
Where had I been dishonest?**		
Where had I been frightened?**		
For what had I been responsible?**		
What decisions did I make based on self that later placed me in a position to be hurt?*		
When in the past did I make this decision? * (Earliest memory)		
Where was I wrong,** what was my part?		

STEPS 6 & 7 – List of Character Defects			

STEP 9 - Amends	STEP 8
	❏ Now ❏ Later ❏ Never

188   FOUR COLUMN INVENTORY...

COLUMN WORK

Resentment and/or Fear: (1)	The Cause (Column 2)	Affects Our: (Column 3)
Person, Place or Thing		☐ Self-Esteem ☐ Security ☐ Ambitions ☐ Personal Relations ☐ Sex Relations ☐ Pride/Shame ☐ Fear
Ask Ourselves: ** (AA 67.3) * (AA 62.2)	Putting out of our mind the wrong others had done, we resolutely looked for our own mistakes… We admitted our wrongs honestly…** **STEPS 4** and/or **10 - (Column 4)**	
Where had I been selfish, self-centred or self-seeking?**		
Where had I been dishonest?**		
Where had I been frightened?**		
For what had I been responsible?**		
What decisions did I make based on self that later placed me in a position to be hurt?*		
When in the past did I make this decision? * (Earliest memory)		
Where was I wrong,** what was my part?		

STEPS 6 & 7 – List of Character Defects			

STEP 9 - Amends	STEP 8
	☐ Now ☐ Later ☐ Never

FORMS ONLY

INVENTORY FORMS

Resentment (1) and/or Fear:	The Cause (Column 2)	Affects Our: (Column 3)
Person, Place or Thing		☐ Self-Esteem ☐ Security ☐ Ambitions ☐ Personal Relations ☐ Sex Relations ☐ Pride/Shame ☐ Fear
Ask Ourselves: ** (AA 67.3) * (AA 62.2)	Putting out of our mind the wrong others had done, we resolutely looked for our own mistakes… We admitted our wrongs honestly…** **STEPS 4** and/or **10 - (Column 4)**	
Where had I been selfish, self-centred or self-seeking?**		
Where had I been dishonest?**		
Where had I been frightened?**		
For what had I been responsible?**		
What decisions did I make based on self that later placed me in a position to be hurt?*		
When in the past did I make this decision? * (Earliest memory)		
Where was I wrong,** what was my part?		

STEPS 6 & 7 – List of Character Defects			

STEP 9 - Amends	STEP 8
	☐ Now ☐ Later ☐ Never

COLUMN WORK

Resentment (1) and/or Fear:	The Cause (Column 2)	Affects Our: (Column 3)
Person, Place or Thing		☐ Self-Esteem ☐ Security ☐ Ambitions ☐ Personal Relations ☐ Sex Relations ☐ Pride/Shame ☐ Fear
Ask Ourselves: ** (AA 67.3) * (AA 62.2)	Putting out of our mind the wrong others had done, we resolutely looked for our own mistakes... We admitted our wrongs honestly...** **STEPS 4 and/or 10 - (Column 4)**	
Where had I been selfish, self-centred or self-seeking?**		
Where had I been dishonest?**		
Where had I been frightened?**		
For what had I been responsible?**		
What decisions did I make based on self that later placed me in a position to be hurt?*		
When in the past did I make this decision? * (Earliest memory)		
Where was I wrong,** what was my part?		

STEPS 6 & 7 – List of Character Defects			

STEP 9 - Amends		STEP 8
		☐ Now ☐ Later ☐ Never

FORMS ONLY

INVENTORY FORMS

Resentment (1) and/or Fear:	The Cause (Column 2)	Affects Our: (Column 3)
Person, Place or Thing		☐ Self-Esteem ☐ Security ☐ Ambitions ☐ Personal Relations ☐ Sex Relations ☐ Pride/Shame ☐ Fear
Ask Ourselves: ** (AA 67.3) * (AA 62.2)	Putting out of our mind the wrong others had done, we resolutely looked for our own mistakes... We admitted our wrongs honestly...** **STEPS 4 and/or 10 - (Column 4)**	
Where had I been selfish, self-centred or self-seeking?**		
Where had I been dishonest?**		
Where had I been frightened?**		
For what had I been responsible?**		
What decisions did I make based on self that later placed me in a position to be hurt?*		
When in the past did I make this decision? * (Earliest memory)		
Where was I wrong,** what was my part?		
STEPS 6 & 7 – List of Character Defects			
STEP 9 - Amends			**STEP 8**
			☐ Now ☐ Later ☐ Never

COLUMN WORK

Resentment (1) and/or Fear:	The Cause (Column 2)	Affects Our: (Column 3)
Person, Place or Thing		☐ Self-Esteem ☐ Security ☐ Ambitions ☐ Personal Relations ☐ Sex Relations ☐ Pride/Shame ☐ Fear
Ask Ourselves: ** (AA 67.3) * (AA 62.2)	Putting out of our mind the wrong others had done, we resolutely looked for our own mistakes... We admitted our wrongs honestly... ** **STEPS 4** and/or **10** - **(Column 4)**	
Where had I been selfish, self-centred or self-seeking?**		
Where had I been dishonest?**		
Where had I been frightened?**		
For what had I been responsible?**		
What decisions did I make based on self that later placed me in a position to be hurt?*		
When in the past did I make this decision? * (Earliest memory)		
Where was I wrong,** what was my part?		

STEPS 6 & 7 – List of Character Defects				

STEP 9 - Amends	STEP 8
	☐ Now ☐ Later ☐ Never

FORMS ONLY

INVENTORY FORMS

Resentment (1) and/or Fear:	The Cause (Column 2)	Affects Our: (Column 3)
Person, Place or Thing		☐ Self-Esteem ☐ Security ☐ Ambitions ☐ Personal Relations ☐ Sex Relations ☐ Pride/Shame ☐ Fear
Ask Ourselves: ** (AA 67.3) * (AA 62.2)	Putting out of our mind the wrong others had done, we resolutely looked for our own mistakes... We admitted our wrongs honestly...** **STEPS 4 and/or 10 - (Column 4)**	
Where had I been selfish, self-centred or self-seeking?**		
Where had I been dishonest?**		
Where had I been frightened?**		
For what had I been responsible?**		
What decisions did I make based on self that later placed me in a position to be hurt?*		
When in the past did I make this decision? * (Earliest memory)		
Where was I wrong,** what was my part?		

STEPS 6 & 7 – List of Character Defects			

STEP 9 - Amends		STEP 8
		☐ Now ☐ Later ☐ Never

FOUR COLUMN INVENTORY...

COLUMN WORK

Resentment (1) and/or Fear:	The Cause (Column 2)	Affects Our: (Column 3)
Person, Place or Thing		☐ Self-Esteem ☐ Security ☐ Ambitions ☐ Personal Relations ☐ Sex Relations ☐ Pride/Shame ☐ Fear
Ask Ourselves: ** (AA 67.3) * (AA 62.2)	Putting out of our mind the wrong others had done, we resolutely looked for our own mistakes… We admitted our wrongs honestly… ** **STEPS 4** and/or **10 - (Column 4)**	
Where had I been selfish, self-centred or self-seeking?**		
Where had I been dishonest?**		
Where had I been frightened?**		
For what had I been responsible?**		
What decisions did I make based on self that later placed me in a position to be hurt?*		
When in the past did I make this decision? * (Earliest memory)		
Where was I wrong,** what was my part?		

STEPS 6 & 7 – List of Character Defects				

STEP 9 - Amends	STEP 8
	☐ Now ☐ Later ☐ Never

FORMS ONLY

INVENTORY FORMS

Resentment (1) and/or Fear:	The Cause (Column 2)	Affects Our: (Column 3)
Person, Place or Thing		☐ Self-Esteem ☐ Security ☐ Ambitions ☐ Personal Relations ☐ Sex Relations ☐ Pride/Shame ☐ Fear
Ask Ourselves: ** (AA 67.3) * (AA 62.2)	Putting out of our mind the wrong others had done, we resolutely looked for our own mistakes... We admitted our wrongs honestly...** **STEPS 4** and/or **10 - (Column 4)**	
Where had I been selfish, self-centred or self-seeking?**		
Where had I been dishonest?**		
Where had I been frightened?**		
For what had I been responsible?**		
What decisions did I make based on self that later placed me in a position to be hurt?*		
When in the past did I make this decision? * (Earliest memory)		
Where was I wrong,** what was my part?		
STEPS 6 & 7 – List of Character Defects		
STEP 9 - Amends		**STEP 8**
		☐ Now ☐ Later ☐ Never

196 FOUR COLUMN INVENTORY...

COLUMN WORK

Resentment (1) and/or Fear:	The Cause (Column 2)	Affects Our: (Column 3)
Person, Place or Thing		☐ Self-Esteem ☐ Security ☐ Ambitions ☐ Personal Relations ☐ Sex Relations ☐ Pride/Shame ☐ Fear
Ask Ourselves: ** (AA 67.3) * (AA 62.2)	Putting out of our mind the wrong others had done, we resolutely looked for our own mistakes… We admitted our wrongs honestly…** **STEPS 4** and/or **10** - **(Column 4)**	
Where had I been selfish, self-centred or self-seeking?**		
Where had I been dishonest?**		
Where had I been frightened?**		
For what had I been responsible?**		
What decisions did I make based on self that later placed me in a position to be hurt?*		
When in the past did I make this decision? * (Earliest memory)		
Where was I wrong,** what was my part?		

STEPS 6 & 7 – List of Character Defects				

STEP 9 - Amends	STEP 8
	☐ Now ☐ Later ☐ Never

INVENTORY FORMS

Resentment (1) and/or Fear:	The Cause (Column 2)	Affects Our: (Column 3)
Person, Place or Thing		☐ Self-Esteem ☐ Security ☐ Ambitions ☐ Personal Relations ☐ Sex Relations ☐ Pride/Shame ☐ Fear
Ask Ourselves: ** (AA 67.3) * (AA 62.2)	Putting out of our mind the wrong others had done, we resolutely looked for our own mistakes... We admitted our wrongs honestly...** **STEPS 4** and/or **10 - (Column 4)**	
Where had I been selfish, self-centred or self-seeking?**		
Where had I been dishonest?**		
Where had I been frightened?**		
For what had I been responsible?**		
What decisions did I make based on self that later placed me in a position to be hurt?*		
When in the past did I make this decision? * (Earliest memory)		
Where was I wrong,** what was my part?		
STEPS 6 & 7 – List of Character Defects		
STEP 9 - Amends		**STEP 8**
		☐ Now ☐ Later ☐ Never

FOUR COLUMN INVENTORY...

COLUMN WORK

Resentment (1) and/or Fear:	The Cause (Column 2)	Affects Our: (Column 3)
Person, Place or Thing		☐ Self-Esteem ☐ Security ☐ Ambitions ☐ Personal Relations ☐ Sex Relations ☐ Pride/Shame ☐ Fear
Ask Ourselves: ** (AA 67.3) * (AA 62.2)	Putting out of our mind the wrong others had done, we resolutely looked for our own mistakes… We admitted our wrongs honestly… ** **STEPS 4** and/or **10 - (Column 4)**	
Where had I been selfish, self-centred or self-seeking?**		
Where had I been dishonest?**		
Where had I been frightened?**		
For what had I been responsible?**		
What decisions did I make based on self that later placed me in a position to be hurt?*		
When in the past did I make this decision? * (Earliest memory)		
Where was I wrong,** what was my part?		

STEPS 6 & 7 – List of Character Defects				

STEP 9 - Amends	STEP 8
	☐ Now ☐ Later ☐ Never

INVENTORY FORMS

Resentment (1) and/or Fear:	The Cause (Column 2)	Affects Our: (Column 3)
Person, Place or Thing		☐ Self-Esteem ☐ Security ☐ Ambitions ☐ Personal Relations ☐ Sex Relations ☐ Pride/Shame ☐ Fear
Ask Ourselves: ** (AA 67.3) * (AA 62.2)	Putting out of our mind the wrong others had done, we resolutely looked for our own mistakes... We admitted our wrongs honestly...** **STEPS 4** and/or **10** - **(Column 4)**	
Where had I been selfish, self-centred or self-seeking?**		
Where had I been dishonest?**		
Where had I been frightened?**		
For what had I been responsible?**		
What decisions did I make based on self that later placed me in a position to be hurt?*		
When in the past did I make this decision? * (Earliest memory)		
Where was I wrong,** what was my part?		
STEPS 6 & 7 – List of Character Defects		
STEP 9 - Amends		**STEP 8**
		☐ **Now** ☐ **Later** ☐ **Never**

200   FOUR COLUMN INVENTORY...

COLUMN WORK

Resentment and/or Fear: (1)	The Cause (Column 2)	Affects Our: (Column 3)
Person, Place or Thing		☐ Self-Esteem ☐ Security ☐ Ambitions ☐ Personal Relations ☐ Sex Relations ☐ Pride/Shame ☐ Fear
Ask Ourselves: ** (AA 67.3) * (AA 62.2)	Putting out of our mind the wrong others had done, we resolutely looked for our own mistakes… We admitted our wrongs honestly…** **STEPS 4** and/or **10** - **(Column 4)**	
Where had I been selfish, self-centred or self-seeking?**		
Where had I been dishonest?**		
Where had I been frightened?**		
For what had I been responsible?**		
What decisions did I make based on self that later placed me in a position to be hurt?*		
When in the past did I make this decision? * (Earliest memory)		
Where was I wrong,** what was my part?		
STEPS 6 & 7 – List of Character Defects		
STEP 9 - Amends		**STEP 8**
		☐ Now ☐ Later ☐ Never

FORMS ONLY

INVENTORY FORMS

Resentment (1) and/or Fear:	The Cause (Column 2)	Affects Our: (Column 3)
Person, Place or Thing		☐ Self-Esteem ☐ Security ☐ Ambitions ☐ Personal Relations ☐ Sex Relations ☐ Pride/Shame ☐ Fear
Ask Ourselves: ** (AA 67.3) * (AA 62.2)	Putting out of our mind the wrong others had done, we resolutely looked for our own mistakes... We admitted our wrongs honestly...** **STEPS 4** and/or **10 - (Column 4)**	
Where had I been selfish, self-centred or self-seeking?**		
Where had I been dishonest?**		
Where had I been frightened?**		
For what had I been responsible?**		
What decisions did I make based on self that later placed me in a position to be hurt?*		
When in the past did I make this decision? * (Earliest memory)		
Where was I wrong,** what was my part?		

STEPS 6 & 7 – List of Character Defects			

STEP 9 - Amends			STEP 8
			☐ Now ☐ Later ☐ **Never**

FOUR COLUMN INVENTORY...

COLUMN WORK

Resentment (1) and/or Fear:	The Cause (Column 2)	Affects Our: (Column 3)
Person, Place or Thing		☐ Self-Esteem ☐ Security ☐ Ambitions ☐ Personal Relations ☐ Sex Relations ☐ Pride/Shame ☐ Fear
Ask Ourselves: ** (AA 67.3) * (AA 62.2)	Putting out of our mind the wrong others had done, we resolutely looked for our own mistakes... We admitted our wrongs honestly...** **STEPS 4 and/or 10 - (Column 4)**	
Where had I been selfish, self-centred or self-seeking?**		
Where had I been dishonest?**		
Where had I been frightened?**		
For what had I been responsible?**		
What decisions did I make based on self that later placed me in a position to be hurt?*		
When in the past did I make this decision? * (Earliest memory)		
Where was I wrong,** what was my part?		

STEPS 6 & 7 – List of Character Defects				

STEP 9 - Amends		STEP 8
		☐ **Now** ☐ **Later** ☐ **Never**

FORMS ONLY

INVENTORY FORMS

Resentment (1) and/or Fear:	The Cause (Column 2)	Affects Our: (Column 3)
Person, Place or Thing		☐ Self-Esteem ☐ Security ☐ Ambitions ☐ Personal Relations ☐ Sex Relations ☐ Pride/Shame ☐ Fear
Ask Ourselves: ** (AA 67.3) * (AA 62.2)	Putting out of our mind the wrong others had done, we resolutely looked for our own mistakes... We admitted our wrongs honestly...** **STEPS 4** and/or **10 - (Column 4)**	
Where had I been selfish, self-centred or self-seeking?**		
Where had I been dishonest?**		
Where had I been frightened?**		
For what had I been responsible?**		
What decisions did I make based on self that later placed me in a position to be hurt?*		
When in the past did I make this decision? * (Earliest memory)		
Where was I wrong,** what was my part?		

STEPS 6 & 7 – List of Character Defects			

STEP 9 - Amends	STEP 8
	☐ **Now** ☐ **Later** ☐ **Never**

204   FOUR COLUMN INVENTORY...

COLUMN WORK

Resentment (1) and/or Fear:	The Cause (Column 2)	Affects Our: (Column 3)
Person, Place or Thing		☐ Self-Esteem ☐ Security ☐ Ambitions ☐ Personal Relations ☐ Sex Relations ☐ Pride/Shame ☐ Fear
Ask Ourselves: ** (AA 67.3) * (AA 62.2)	Putting out of our mind the wrong others had done, we resolutely looked for our own mistakes… We admitted our wrongs honestly…** **STEPS 4 and/or 10 - (Column 4)**	
Where had I been selfish, self-centred or self-seeking?**		
Where had I been dishonest?**		
Where had I been frightened?**		
For what had I been responsible?**		
What decisions did I make based on self that later placed me in a position to be hurt?*		
When in the past did I make this decision? * (Earliest memory)		
Where was I wrong,** what was my part?		

STEPS 6 & 7 – List of Character Defects			

STEP 9 - Amends	STEP 8
	☐ Now ☐ Later ☐ Never

FORMS ONLY

INVENTORY FORMS

Resentment (1) and/or Fear:	The Cause (Column 2)	Affects Our: (Column 3)
Person, Place or Thing		☐ Self-Esteem ☐ Security ☐ Ambitions ☐ Personal Relations ☐ Sex Relations ☐ Pride/Shame ☐ Fear
Ask Ourselves: ** (AA 67.3) * (AA 62.2)	Putting out of our mind the wrong others had done, we resolutely looked for our own mistakes... We admitted our wrongs honestly...** **STEPS 4** and/or **10** - **(Column 4)**	
Where had I been selfish, self-centred or self-seeking?**		
Where had I been dishonest?**		
Where had I been frightened?**		
For what had I been responsible?**		
What decisions did I make based on self that later placed me in a position to be hurt?*		
When in the past did I make this decision? * (Earliest memory)		
Where was I wrong,** what was my part?		

STEPS 6 & 7 – List of Character Defects			

STEP 9 - Amends	STEP 8
	☐ Now ☐ Later ☐ Never

COLUMN WORK

Resentment and/or Fear: (1)	The Cause (Column 2)	Affects Our: (Column 3)
Person, Place or Thing		☐ Self-Esteem ☐ Security ☐ Ambitions ☐ Personal Relations ☐ Sex Relations ☐ Pride/Shame ☐ Fear
Ask Ourselves: ** (AA 67.3) * (AA 62.2)	Putting out of our mind the wrong others had done, we resolutely looked for our own mistakes... We admitted our wrongs honestly...** **STEPS 4** and/or **10** - **(Column 4)**	
Where had I been selfish, self-centred or self-seeking?**		
Where had I been dishonest?**		
Where had I been frightened?**		
For what had I been responsible?**		
What decisions did I make based on self that later placed me in a position to be hurt?*		
When in the past did I make this decision? * (Earliest memory)		
Where was I wrong,** what was my part?		

STEPS 6 & 7 – List of Character Defects

STEP 9 - Amends	STEP 8
	☐ Now ☐ Later ☐ Never

INVENTORY FORMS

Resentment (1) and/or Fear:	The Cause (Column 2)	Affects Our: (Column 3)
Person, Place or Thing		☐ Self-Esteem ☐ Security ☐ Ambitions ☐ Personal Relations ☐ Sex Relations ☐ Pride/Shame ☐ Fear
Ask Ourselves: ** (AA 67.3) * (AA 62.2)	Putting out of our mind the wrong others had done, we resolutely looked for our own mistakes... We admitted our wrongs honestly...** **STEPS 4** and/or **10 - (Column 4)**	
Where had I been selfish, self-centred or self-seeking?**		
Where had I been dishonest?**		
Where had I been frightened?**		
For what had I been responsible?**		
What decisions did I make based on self that later placed me in a position to be hurt?*		
When in the past did I make this decision? * (Earliest memory)		
Where was I wrong,** what was my part?		
STEPS 6 & 7 – List of Character Defects		
STEP 9 - Amends		**STEP 8**
		☐ Now ☐ Later ☐ Never

FOUR COLUMN INVENTORY...

COLUMN WORK

Resentment (1) and/or Fear:	The Cause (Column 2)	Affects Our: (Column 3)
Person, Place or Thing		☐ Self-Esteem ☐ Security ☐ Ambitions ☐ Personal Relations ☐ Sex Relations ☐ Pride/Shame ☐ Fear
Ask Ourselves: ** (AA 67.3) * (AA 62.2)	Putting out of our mind the wrong others had done, we resolutely looked for our own mistakes… We admitted our wrongs honestly…** **STEPS** 4 and/or 10 - **(Column 4)**	
Where had I been selfish, self-centred or self-seeking?**		
Where had I been dishonest?**		
Where had I been frightened?**		
For what had I been responsible?**		
What decisions did I make based on self that later placed me in a position to be hurt?*		
When in the past did I make this decision? * (Earliest memory)		
Where was I wrong,** what was my part?		

STEPS 6 & 7 – List of Character Defects			

STEP 9 - Amends	STEP 8
	☐ Now ☐ Later ☐ Never

FORMS ONLY

INVENTORY FORMS

Resentment (1) and/or Fear:	The Cause (Column 2)	Affects Our: (Column 3)
Person, Place or Thing		☐ Self-Esteem ☐ Security ☐ Ambitions ☐ Personal Relations ☐ Sex Relations ☐ Pride/Shame ☐ Fear
Ask Ourselves: ** (AA 67.3) * (AA 62.2)	Putting out of our mind the wrong others had done, we resolutely looked for our own mistakes… We admitted our wrongs honestly…** **STEPS 4 and/or 10 - (Column 4)**	
Where had I been selfish, self-centred or self-seeking?**		
Where had I been dishonest?**		
Where had I been frightened?**		
For what had I been responsible?**		
What decisions did I make based on self that later placed me in a position to be hurt?*		
When in the past did I make this decision? * (Earliest memory)		
Where was I wrong,** what was my part?		

STEPS 6 & 7 – List of Character Defects

STEP 9 - Amends	STEP 8
	☐ Now ☐ Later ☐ Never

FOUR COLUMN INVENTORY…

COLUMN WORK

Resentment (1) and/or Fear:	The Cause (Column 2)	Affects Our: (Column 3)
Person, Place or Thing		☐ Self-Esteem ☐ Security ☐ Ambitions ☐ Personal Relations ☐ Sex Relations ☐ Pride/Shame ☐ Fear
Ask Ourselves: ** (AA 67.3) * (AA 62.2)	Putting out of our mind the wrong others had done, we resolutely looked for our own mistakes… We admitted our wrongs honestly…** **STEPS 4** and/or **10** - **(Column 4)**	
Where had I been selfish, self-centred or self-seeking?**		
Where had I been dishonest?**		
Where had I been frightened?**		
For what had I been responsible?**		
What decisions did I make based on self that later placed me in a position to be hurt?*		
When in the past did I make this decision? * (Earliest memory)		
Where was I wrong,** what was my part?		
STEPS 6 & 7 – List of Character Defects					
STEP 9 - Amends					**STEP 8**
					☐ Now ☐ Later ☐ Never

INVENTORY FORMS

Resentment (1) and/or Fear:	The Cause (Column 2)	Affects Our: (Column 3)
Person, Place or Thing		☐ Self-Esteem ☐ Security ☐ Ambitions ☐ Personal Relations ☐ Sex Relations ☐ Pride/Shame ☐ Fear
Ask Ourselves: ** (AA 67.3) * (AA 62.2)	Putting out of our mind the wrong others had done, we resolutely looked for our own mistakes... We admitted our wrongs honestly...** **STEPS 4** and/or **10 - (Column 4)**	
Where had I been selfish, self-centred or self-seeking?**		
Where had I been dishonest?**		
Where had I been frightened?**		
For what had I been responsible?**		
What decisions did I make based on self that later placed me in a position to be hurt?*		
When in the past did I make this decision? * (Earliest memory)		
Where was I wrong,** what was my part?		

STEPS 6 & 7 – List of Character Defects

STEP 9 - Amends	STEP 8
	☐ Now ☐ Later ☐ Never

FOUR COLUMN INVENTORY...

COLUMN WORK

Resentment and/or Fear: (1)	The Cause (Column 2)	Affects Our: (Column 3)
Person, Place or Thing		☐ Self-Esteem ☐ Security ☐ Ambitions ☐ Personal Relations ☐ Sex Relations ☐ Pride/Shame ☐ Fear
Ask Ourselves: ** (AA 67.3) * (AA 62.2)	Putting out of our mind the wrong others had done, we resolutely looked for our own mistakes... We admitted our wrongs honestly...** **STEPS 4** and/or **10** - **(Column 4)**	
Where had I been selfish, self-centred or self-seeking?**		
Where had I been dishonest?**		
Where had I been frightened?**		
For what had I been responsible?**		
What decisions did I make based on self that later placed me in a position to be hurt?*		
When in the past did I make this decision? * (Earliest memory)		
Where was I wrong,** what was my part?		

STEPS 6 & 7 – List of Character Defects

STEP 9 - Amends	STEP 8
	☐ Now ☐ Later ☐ Never

INVENTORY FORMS

Resentment (1) and/or Fear:	The Cause (Column 2)	Affects Our: (Column 3)
Person, Place or Thing		☐ Self-Esteem ☐ Security ☐ Ambitions ☐ Personal Relations ☐ Sex Relations ☐ Pride/Shame ☐ Fear
Ask Ourselves: ** (AA 67.3) * (AA 62.2)	Putting out of our mind the wrong others had done, we resolutely looked for our own mistakes… We admitted our wrongs honestly…** **STEPS 4** and/or **10 - (Column 4)**	
Where had I been selfish, self-centred or self-seeking?**		
Where had I been dishonest?**		
Where had I been frightened?**		
For what had I been responsible?**		
What decisions did I make based on self that later placed me in a position to be hurt?*		
When in the past did I make this decision? * (Earliest memory)		
Where was I wrong,** what was my part?		

STEPS 6 & 7 – List of Character Defects			

STEP 9 - Amends	STEP 8
	☐ Now ☐ Later ☐ Never

214   FOUR COLUMN INVENTORY…

COLUMN WORK

Resentment (1) and/or Fear:	The Cause (Column 2)	Affects Our: (Column 3)
Person, Place or Thing		☐ Self-Esteem ☐ Security ☐ Ambitions ☐ Personal Relations ☐ Sex Relations ☐ Pride/Shame ☐ Fear
Ask Ourselves: ** (AA 67.3) * (AA 62.2)	Putting out of our mind the wrong others had done, we resolutely looked for our own mistakes… We admitted our wrongs honestly…** **STEPS 4 and/or 10 - (Column 4)**	
Where had I been selfish, self-centred or self-seeking?**		
Where had I been dishonest?**		
Where had I been frightened?**		
For what had I been responsible?**		
What decisions did I make based on self that later placed me in a position to be hurt?*		
When in the past did I make this decision? * (Earliest memory)		
Where was I wrong,** what was my part?		

STEPS 6 & 7 – List of Character Defects				

STEP 9 - Amends	STEP 8
	☐ Now ☐ Later ☐ Never

FORMS ONLY

INVENTORY FORMS

Resentment (1) and/or Fear:	The Cause (Column 2)	Affects Our: (Column 3)
Person, Place or Thing		☐ Self-Esteem ☐ Security ☐ Ambitions ☐ Personal Relations ☐ Sex Relations ☐ Pride/Shame ☐ Fear
Ask Ourselves: ** (AA 67.3) * (AA 62.2)	Putting out of our mind the wrong others had done, we resolutely looked for our own mistakes... We admitted our wrongs honestly...** **STEPS 4 and/or 10 - (Column 4)**	
Where had I been selfish, self-centred or self-seeking?**		
Where had I been dishonest?**		
Where had I been frightened?**		
For what had I been responsible?**		
What decisions did I make based on self that later placed me in a position to be hurt?*		
When in the past did I make this decision? * (Earliest memory)		
Where was I wrong,** what was my part?		

STEPS 6 & 7 – List of Character Defects			

STEP 9 - Amends	STEP 8
	☐ Now ☐ Later ☐ Never

FOUR COLUMN INVENTORY...

COLUMN WORK

Resentment and/or Fear: (1)	The Cause (Column 2)	Affects Our: (Column 3)
Person, Place or Thing		☐ Self-Esteem ☐ Security ☐ Ambitions ☐ Personal Relations ☐ Sex Relations ☐ Pride/Shame ☐ Fear
Ask Ourselves: ** (AA 67.3) * (AA 62.2)	Putting out of our mind the wrong others had done, we resolutely looked for our own mistakes... We admitted our wrongs honestly...** **STEPS 4** and/or **10** - **(Column 4)**	
Where had I been selfish, self-centred or self-seeking?**		
Where had I been dishonest?**		
Where had I been frightened?**		
For what had I been responsible?**		
What decisions did I make based on self that later placed me in a position to be hurt?*		
When in the past did I make this decision? * (Earliest memory)		
Where was I wrong,** what was my part?		

STEPS 6 & 7 – List of Character Defects			

STEP 9 - Amends	STEP 8
	☐ Now ☐ Later ☐ Never

FORMS ONLY

INVENTORY FORMS

Resentment (1) and/or Fear:	The Cause (Column 2)	Affects Our: (Column 3)
Person, Place or Thing		☐ Self-Esteem ☐ Security ☐ Ambitions ☐ Personal Relations ☐ Sex Relations ☐ Pride/Shame ☐ Fear
Ask Ourselves: ** (AA 67.3) * (AA 62.2)	Putting out of our mind the wrong others had done, we resolutely looked for our own mistakes... We admitted our wrongs honestly...** **STEPS 4** and/or **10** - **(Column 4)**	
Where had I been selfish, self-centred or self-seeking?**		
Where had I been dishonest?**		
Where had I been frightened?**		
For what had I been responsible?**		
What decisions did I make based on self that later placed me in a position to be hurt?*		
When in the past did I make this decision? * (Earliest memory)		
Where was I wrong,** what was my part?		

STEPS 6 & 7 – List of Character Defects

STEP 9 - Amends	STEP 8
	☐ Now ☐ Later ☐ Never

FOUR COLUMN INVENTORY...

COLUMN WORK

Resentment (1) and/or Fear:	The Cause (Column 2)	Affects Our: (Column 3)
Person, Place or Thing		☐ Self-Esteem ☐ Security ☐ Ambitions ☐ Personal Relations ☐ Sex Relations ☐ Pride/Shame ☐ Fear
Ask Ourselves: ** (AA 67.3) * (AA 62.2)	Putting out of our mind the wrong others had done, we resolutely looked for our own mistakes... We admitted our wrongs honestly...** **STEPS 4** and/or **10 - (Column 4)**	
Where had I been selfish, self-centred or self-seeking?**		
Where had I been dishonest?**		
Where had I been frightened?**		
For what had I been responsible?**		
What decisions did I make based on self that later placed me in a position to be hurt?*		
When in the past did I make this decision? * (Earliest memory)		
Where was I wrong,** what was my part?		

STEPS 6 & 7 – List of Character Defects				

STEP 9 - Amends	STEP 8
	☐ Now ☐ Later ☐ Never

FORMS ONLY

INVENTORY FORMS

Resentment (1) and/or Fear:	The Cause (Column 2)	Affects Our: (Column 3)
Person, Place or Thing		☐ Self-Esteem ☐ Security ☐ Ambitions ☐ Personal Relations ☐ Sex Relations ☐ Pride/Shame ☐ Fear
Ask Ourselves: ** (AA 67.3) * (AA 62.2)	Putting out of our mind the wrong others had done, we resolutely looked for our own mistakes... We admitted our wrongs honestly...** **STEPS 4** and/or **10 - (Column 4)**	
Where had I been selfish, self-centred or self-seeking?**		
Where had I been dishonest?**		
Where had I been frightened?**		
For what had I been responsible?**		
What decisions did I make based on self that later placed me in a position to be hurt?*		
When in the past did I make this decision? * (Earliest memory)		
Where was I wrong,** what was my part?		

STEPS 6 & 7 – List of Character Defects			

STEP 9 - Amends	STEP 8
	☐ Now ☐ Later ☐ Never

FOUR COLUMN INVENTORY...

COLUMN WORK

Resentment and/or Fear: (1)	The Cause (Column 2)	Affects Our: (Column 3)
Person, Place or Thing		☐ Self-Esteem ☐ Security ☐ Ambitions ☐ Personal Relations ☐ Sex Relations ☐ Pride/Shame ☐ Fear
Ask Ourselves: ** (AA 67.3) * (AA 62.2)	Putting out of our mind the wrong others had done, we resolutely looked for our own mistakes... We admitted our wrongs honestly...** **STEPS 4 and/or 10 - (Column 4)**	
Where had I been selfish, self-centred or self-seeking?**		
Where had I been dishonest?**		
Where had I been frightened?**		
For what had I been responsible?**		
What decisions did I make based on self that later placed me in a position to be hurt?*		
When in the past did I make this decision? * (Earliest memory)		
Where was I wrong,** what was my part?		

STEPS 6 & 7 – List of Character Defects

STEP 9 - Amends | STEP 8

☐ Now
☐ Later
☐ Never

FORMS ONLY

INVENTORY FORMS

Resentment (1) and/or Fear:	The Cause (Column 2)	Affects Our: (Column 3)
Person, Place or Thing		☐ Self-Esteem ☐ Security ☐ Ambitions ☐ Personal Relations ☐ Sex Relations ☐ Pride/Shame ☐ Fear
Ask Ourselves: ** (AA 67.3) * (AA 62.2)	Putting out of our mind the wrong others had done, we resolutely looked for our own mistakes... We admitted our wrongs honestly...** **STEPS 4** and/or **10 - (Column 4)**	
Where had I been selfish, self-centred or self-seeking?**		
Where had I been dishonest?**		
Where had I been frightened?**		
For what had I been responsible?**		
What decisions did I make based on self that later placed me in a position to be hurt?*		
When in the past did I make this decision? * (Earliest memory)		
Where was I wrong,** what was my part?		
STEPS 6 & 7 – List of Character Defects			
STEP 9 - Amends		**STEP 8**
		☐ Now ☐ Later ☐ Never

COLUMN WORK

Resentment and/or Fear: (1)	The Cause (Column 2)	Affects Our: (Column 3)
Person, Place or Thing		☐ Self-Esteem ☐ Security ☐ Ambitions ☐ Personal Relations ☐ Sex Relations ☐ Pride/Shame ☐ Fear
Ask Ourselves: ** (AA 67.3) * (AA 62.2)	Putting out of our mind the wrong others had done, we resolutely looked for our own mistakes… We admitted our wrongs honestly… ** **STEPS 4** and/or **10 - (Column 4)**	
Where had I been selfish, self-centred or self-seeking?**		
Where had I been dishonest?**		
Where had I been frightened?**		
For what had I been responsible?**		
What decisions did I make based on self that later placed me in a position to be hurt?*		
When in the past did I make this decision? * (Earliest memory)		
Where was I wrong,** what was my part?		

STEPS 6 & 7 – List of Character Defects

STEP 9 - Amends | STEP 8

☐ Now
☐ Later
☐ Never

FORMS ONLY

INVENTORY FORMS

Resentment (1) and/or Fear:	The Cause (Column 2)	Affects Our: (Column 3)
Person, Place or Thing		☐ Self-Esteem ☐ Security ☐ Ambitions ☐ Personal Relations ☐ Sex Relations ☐ Pride/Shame ☐ Fear
Ask Ourselves: ** (AA 67.3) * (AA 62.2)	Putting out of our mind the wrong others had done, we resolutely looked for our own mistakes... We admitted our wrongs honestly...** **STEPS 4** and/or **10** - **(Column 4)**	
Where had I been selfish, self-centred or self-seeking?**		
Where had I been dishonest?**		
Where had I been frightened?**		
For what had I been responsible?**		
What decisions did I make based on self that later placed me in a position to be hurt?*		
When in the past did I make this decision? * (Earliest memory)		
Where was I wrong,** what was my part?		
STEPS 6 & 7 – List of Character Defects		
STEP 9 - Amends		**STEP 8**
		☐ **Now** ☐ **Later** ☐ **Never**

224   FOUR COLUMN INVENTORY...

COLUMN WORK

Resentment (1) and/or Fear:	The Cause (Column 2)	Affects Our: (Column 3)
Person, Place or Thing		☐ Self-Esteem ☐ Security ☐ Ambitions ☐ Personal Relations ☐ Sex Relations ☐ Pride/Shame ☐ Fear
Ask Ourselves: ** (AA 67.3) * (AA 62.2)	Putting out of our mind the wrong others had done, we resolutely looked for our own mistakes… We admitted our wrongs honestly…** **STEPS 4** and/or **10** - **(Column 4)**	
Where had I been selfish, self-centred or self-seeking?**		
Where had I been dishonest?**		
Where had I been frightened?**		
For what had I been responsible?**		
What decisions did I make based on self that later placed me in a position to be hurt?*		
When in the past did I make this decision? * (Earliest memory)		
Where was I wrong,** what was my part?		

STEPS 6 & 7 – List of Character Defects

STEP 9 - Amends	STEP 8
	☐ Now ☐ Later ☐ Never

FORMS ONLY

INVENTORY FORMS

Resentment (1) and/or Fear:	The Cause (Column 2)	Affects Our: (Column 3)
Person, Place or Thing		☐ Self-Esteem ☐ Security ☐ Ambitions ☐ Personal Relations ☐ Sex Relations ☐ Pride/Shame ☐ Fear
Ask Ourselves: ** (AA 67.3) * (AA 62.2)	Putting out of our mind the wrong others had done, we resolutely looked for our own mistakes... We admitted our wrongs honestly...** **STEPS 4** and/or **10 - (Column 4)**	
Where had I been selfish, self-centred or self-seeking?**		
Where had I been dishonest?**		
Where had I been frightened?**		
For what had I been responsible?**		
What decisions did I make based on self that later placed me in a position to be hurt?*		
When in the past did I make this decision? * (Earliest memory)		
Where was I wrong,** what was my part?		
STEPS 6 & 7 – List of Character Defects			
STEP 9 - Amends			**STEP 8**
			☐ Now ☐ Later ☐ Never

FOUR COLUMN INVENTORY...

COLUMN WORK

Resentment (1) and/or Fear:	The Cause (Column 2)	Affects Our: (Column 3)
Person, Place or Thing		☐ Self-Esteem ☐ Security ☐ Ambitions ☐ Personal Relations ☐ Sex Relations ☐ Pride/Shame ☐ Fear
Ask Ourselves: ** (AA 67.3) * (AA 62.2)	Putting out of our mind the wrong others had done, we resolutely looked for our own mistakes… We admitted our wrongs honestly…** **STEPS 4 and/or 10 - (Column 4)**	
Where had I been selfish, self-centred or self-seeking?**		
Where had I been dishonest?**		
Where had I been frightened?**		
For what had I been responsible?**		
What decisions did I make based on self that later placed me in a position to be hurt?*		
When in the past did I make this decision? * (Earliest memory)		
Where was I wrong,** what was my part?		

STEPS 6 & 7 – List of Character Defects				

STEP 9 - Amends	STEP 8
	☐ Now ☐ Later ☐ Never

FORMS ONLY

INVENTORY FORMS

Resentment (1) and/or Fear:	The Cause (Column 2)	Affects Our: (Column 3)
Person, Place or Thing		☐ Self-Esteem ☐ Security ☐ Ambitions ☐ Personal Relations ☐ Sex Relations ☐ Pride/Shame ☐ Fear
Ask Ourselves: ** (AA 67.3) * (AA 62.2)	Putting out of our mind the wrong others had done, we resolutely looked for our own mistakes... We admitted our wrongs honestly...** **STEPS 4** and/or **10** - **(Column 4)**	
Where had I been selfish, self-centred or self-seeking?**		
Where had I been dishonest?**		
Where had I been frightened?**		
For what had I been responsible?**		
What decisions did I make based on self that later placed me in a position to be hurt?*		
When in the past did I make this decision? * (Earliest memory)		
Where was I wrong,** what was my part?		

STEPS 6 & 7 – List of Character Defects				

STEP 9 - Amends	STEP 8
	☐ Now ☐ Later ☐ Never

FOUR COLUMN INVENTORY...

COLUMN WORK

Resentment (1) and/or Fear:	The Cause (Column 2)	Affects Our: (Column 3)
Person, Place or Thing		☐ Self-Esteem ☐ Security ☐ Ambitions ☐ Personal Relations ☐ Sex Relations ☐ Pride/Shame ☐ Fear
Ask Ourselves: ** (AA 67.3) * (AA 62.2)	Putting out of our mind the wrong others had done, we resolutely looked for our own mistakes… We admitted our wrongs honestly…** **STEPS 4** and/or **10 - (Column 4)**	
Where had I been selfish, self-centred or self-seeking?**		
Where had I been dishonest?**		
Where had I been frightened?**		
For what had I been responsible?**		
What decisions did I make based on self that later placed me in a position to be hurt?*		
When in the past did I make this decision? * (Earliest memory)		
Where was I wrong,** what was my part?		

STEPS 6 & 7 – List of Character Defects				

STEP 9 - Amends	STEP 8
	☐ Now ☐ Later ☐ Never

FORMS ONLY

INVENTORY FORMS

Resentment (1) and/or Fear:	The Cause (Column 2)	Affects Our: (Column 3)
Person, Place or Thing		☐ Self-Esteem ☐ Security ☐ Ambitions ☐ Personal Relations ☐ Sex Relations ☐ Pride/Shame ☐ Fear
Ask Ourselves: ** (AA 67.3) * (AA 62.2)	Putting out of our mind the wrong others had done, we resolutely looked for our own mistakes… We admitted our wrongs honestly…** **STEPS 4** and/or **10 - (Column 4)**	
Where had I been selfish, self-centred or self-seeking?**		
Where had I been dishonest?**		
Where had I been frightened?**		
For what had I been responsible?**		
What decisions did I make based on self that later placed me in a position to be hurt?*		
When in the past did I make this decision? * (Earliest memory)		
Where was I wrong,** what was my part?		
STEPS 6 & 7 – List of Character Defects		
STEP 9 - Amends		**STEP 8**
		☐ Now ☐ Later ☐ Never

FOUR COLUMN INVENTORY…

COLUMN WORK

Resentment (1) and/or Fear:	The Cause (Column 2)	Affects Our: (Column 3)
Person, Place or Thing		☐ Self-Esteem ☐ Security ☐ Ambitions ☐ Personal Relations ☐ Sex Relations ☐ Pride/Shame ☐ Fear
Ask Ourselves: ** (AA 67.3) * (AA 62.2)	Putting out of our mind the wrong others had done, we resolutely looked for our own mistakes... We admitted our wrongs honestly...** STEPS 4 and/or 10 - (Column 4)	
Where had I been selfish, self-centred or self-seeking?**		
Where had I been dishonest?**		
Where had I been frightened?**		
For what had I been responsible?**		
What decisions did I make based on self that later placed me in a position to be hurt?*		
When in the past did I make this decision? * (Earliest memory)		
Where was I wrong,** what was my part?		

STEPS 6 & 7 – List of Character Defects			

STEP 9 - Amends	STEP 8
	☐ Now ☐ Later ☐ Never

INVENTORY FORMS

Resentment (1) and/or Fear:	The Cause (Column 2)	Affects Our: (Column 3)
Person, Place or Thing		☐ Self-Esteem ☐ Security ☐ Ambitions ☐ Personal Relations ☐ Sex Relations ☐ Pride/Shame ☐ Fear
Ask Ourselves: ** (AA 67.3) * (AA 62.2)	Putting out of our mind the wrong others had done, we resolutely looked for our own mistakes… We admitted our wrongs honestly…** **STEPS 4** and/or **10 - (Column 4)**	
Where had I been selfish, self-centred or self-seeking?**		
Where had I been dishonest?**		
Where had I been frightened?**		
For what had I been responsible?**		
What decisions did I make based on self that later placed me in a position to be hurt?*		
When in the past did I make this decision? * (Earliest memory)		
Where was I wrong,** what was my part?		
STEPS 6 & 7 – List of Character Defects		
STEP 9 - Amends		**STEP 8**
		☐ Now ☐ Later ☐ Never

232 FOUR COLUMN INVENTORY…

COLUMN WORK

Resentment (1) and/or Fear:	The Cause (Column 2)	Affects Our: (Column 3)
Person, Place or Thing		☐ Self-Esteem ☐ Security ☐ Ambitions ☐ Personal Relations ☐ Sex Relations ☐ Pride/Shame ☐ Fear
Ask Ourselves: ** (AA 67.3) * (AA 62.2)	Putting out of our mind the wrong others had done, we resolutely looked for our own mistakes… We admitted our wrongs honestly…** **STEPS 4 and/or 10 - (Column 4)**	
Where had I been selfish, self-centred or self-seeking?**		
Where had I been dishonest?**		
Where had I been frightened?**		
For what had I been responsible?**		
What decisions did I make based on self that later placed me in a position to be hurt?*		
When in the past did I make this decision? * (Earliest memory)		
Where was I wrong,** what was my part?		
STEPS 6 & 7 – List of Character Defects		

STEP 9 - Amends	STEP 8
	☐ Now ☐ Later ☐ Never

INVENTORY FORMS

Resentment (1) and/or Fear:	The Cause (Column 2)	Affects Our: (Column 3)
Person, Place or Thing		☐ Self-Esteem ☐ Security ☐ Ambitions ☐ Personal Relations ☐ Sex Relations ☐ Pride/Shame ☐ Fear
Ask Ourselves: ** (AA 67.3) * (AA 62.2)	Putting out of our mind the wrong others had done, we resolutely looked for our own mistakes... We admitted our wrongs honestly...** **STEPS 4** and/or **10** - **(Column 4)**	
Where had I been selfish, self-centred or self-seeking?**		
Where had I been dishonest?**		
Where had I been frightened?**		
For what had I been responsible?**		
What decisions did I make based on self that later placed me in a position to be hurt?*		
When in the past did I make this decision? * (Earliest memory)		
Where was I wrong,** what was my part?		
STEPS 6 & 7 – List of Character Defects		
STEP 9 - Amends		**STEP 8**
		☐ Now ☐ Later ☐ Never

COLUMN WORK

Resentment (1) and/or Fear:	The Cause (Column 2)	Affects Our: (Column 3)
Person, Place or Thing		☐ Self-Esteem ☐ Security ☐ Ambitions ☐ Personal Relations ☐ Sex Relations ☐ Pride/Shame ☐ Fear
Ask Ourselves: ** (AA 67.3) * (AA 62.2)	Putting out of our mind the wrong others had done, we resolutely looked for our own mistakes… We admitted our wrongs honestly…** **STEPS 4** and/or **10** - **(Column 4)**	
Where had I been selfish, self-centred or self-seeking?**		
Where had I been dishonest?**		
Where had I been frightened?**		
For what had I been responsible?**		
What decisions did I make based on self that later placed me in a position to be hurt?*		
When in the past did I make this decision? * (Earliest memory)		
Where was I wrong,** what was my part?		

STEPS 6 & 7 – List of Character Defects			

STEP 9 - Amends	STEP 8
	☐ Now ☐ Later ☐ Never

FORMS ONLY

INVENTORY FORMS

Resentment (1) and/or Fear:	The Cause (Column 2)	Affects Our: (Column 3)
Person, Place or Thing		☐ Self-Esteem ☐ Security ☐ Ambitions ☐ Personal Relations ☐ Sex Relations ☐ Pride/Shame ☐ Fear
Ask Ourselves: ** (AA 67.3) * (AA 62.2)	Putting out of our mind the wrong others had done, we resolutely looked for our own mistakes... We admitted our wrongs honestly... ** **STEPS 4** and/or **10** - **(Column 4)**	
Where had I been selfish, self-centred or self-seeking?**		
Where had I been dishonest?**		
Where had I been frightened?**		
For what had I been responsible?**		
What decisions did I make based on self that later placed me in a position to be hurt?*		
When in the past did I make this decision? * (Earliest memory)		
Where was I wrong,** what was my part?		
STEPS 6 & 7 – List of Character Defects			
STEP 9 - Amends		**STEP 8**
		☐ Now ☐ Later ☐ Never

COLUMN WORK

Resentment (1) and/or Fear:	The Cause (Column 2)	Affects Our: (Column 3)
Person, Place or Thing		☐ Self-Esteem ☐ Security ☐ Ambitions ☐ Personal Relations ☐ Sex Relations ☐ Pride/Shame ☐ Fear
Ask Ourselves: ** (AA 67.3) * (AA 62.2)	Putting out of our mind the wrong others had done, we resolutely looked for our own mistakes... We admitted our wrongs honestly...** **STEPS 4** and/or **10 - (Column 4)**	
Where had I been selfish, self-centred or self-seeking?**		
Where had I been dishonest?**		
Where had I been frightened?**		
For what had I been responsible?**		
What decisions did I make based on self that later placed me in a position to be hurt?*		
When in the past did I make this decision? * (Earliest memory)		
Where was I wrong,** what was my part?		

STEPS 6 & 7 – List of Character Defects					

STEP 9 - Amends	STEP 8
	☐ Now ☐ Later ☐ Never

FORMS ONLY

INVENTORY FORMS

Resentment (1) and/or Fear:	The Cause (Column 2)	Affects Our: (Column 3)
Person, Place or Thing		☐ Self-Esteem ☐ Security ☐ Ambitions ☐ Personal Relations ☐ Sex Relations ☐ Pride/Shame ☐ Fear
Ask Ourselves: ** (AA 67.3) * (AA 62.2)	Putting out of our mind the wrong others had done, we resolutely looked for our own mistakes... We admitted our wrongs honestly...** **STEPS 4** and/or **10** - **(Column 4)**	
Where had I been selfish, self-centred or self-seeking?**		
Where had I been dishonest?**		
Where had I been frightened?**		
For what had I been responsible?**		
What decisions did I make based on self that later placed me in a position to be hurt?*		
When in the past did I make this decision? * (Earliest memory)		
Where was I wrong,** what was my part?		

STEPS 6 & 7 – List of Character Defects			

STEP 9 - Amends	STEP 8
	☐ Now ☐ Later ☐ Never

COLUMN WORK

Resentment (1) and/or Fear:	The Cause (Column 2)	Affects Our: (Column 3)
Person, Place or Thing		☐ Self-Esteem ☐ Security ☐ Ambitions ☐ Personal Relations ☐ Sex Relations ☐ Pride/Shame ☐ Fear
Ask Ourselves: ** (AA 67.3) * (AA 62.2)	Putting out of our mind the wrong others had done, we resolutely looked for our own mistakes… We admitted our wrongs honestly…** **STEPS 4 and/or 10 - (Column 4)**	
Where had I been selfish, self-centred or self-seeking?**		
Where had I been dishonest?**		
Where had I been frightened?**		
For what had I been responsible?**		
What decisions did I make based on self that later placed me in a position to be hurt?*		
When in the past did I make this decision? * (Earliest memory)		
Where was I wrong,** what was my part?		

STEPS 6 & 7 – List of Character Defects			

STEP 9 - Amends	STEP 8
	☐ Now ☐ Later ☐ Never

FORMS ONLY

INVENTORY FORMS

Resentment (1) and/or Fear:	The Cause (Column 2)	Affects Our: (Column 3)
Person, Place or Thing		☐ Self-Esteem ☐ Security ☐ Ambitions ☐ Personal Relations ☐ Sex Relations ☐ Pride/Shame ☐ Fear
Ask Ourselves: ** (AA 67.3) * (AA 62.2)	Putting out of our mind the wrong others had done, we resolutely looked for our own mistakes... We admitted our wrongs honestly...** **STEPS 4** and/or **10** - **(Column 4)**	
Where had I been selfish, self-centred or self-seeking?**		
Where had I been dishonest?**		
Where had I been frightened?**		
For what had I been responsible?**		
What decisions did I make based on self that later placed me in a position to be hurt?*		
When in the past did I make this decision? * (Earliest memory)		
Where was I wrong,** what was my part?		

STEPS 6 & 7 – List of Character Defects				

STEP 9 - Amends	STEP 8
	☐ **Now** ☐ **Later** ☐ **Never**

FOUR COLUMN INVENTORY...

COLUMN WORK

Resentment and/or Fear: (1)	The Cause (Column 2)	Affects Our: (Column 3)
Person, Place or Thing		☐ Self-Esteem ☐ Security ☐ Ambitions ☐ Personal Relations ☐ Sex Relations ☐ Pride/Shame ☐ Fear
Ask Ourselves: ** (AA 67.3) * (AA 62.2)	Putting out of our mind the wrong others had done, we resolutely looked for our own mistakes… We admitted our wrongs honestly…** **STEPS 4** and/or **10 - (Column 4)**	
Where had I been selfish, self-centred or self-seeking?**		
Where had I been dishonest?**		
Where had I been frightened?**		
For what had I been responsible?**		
What decisions did I make based on self that later placed me in a position to be hurt?*		
When in the past did I make this decision? * (Earliest memory)		
Where was I wrong,** what was my part?		

STEPS 6 & 7 – List of Character Defects

STEP 9 - Amends	STEP 8
	☐ Now ☐ Later ☐ Never

FORMS ONLY

INVENTORY FORMS

Resentment (1) and/or Fear:	The Cause (Column 2)	Affects Our: (Column 3)
Person, Place or Thing		☐ Self-Esteem ☐ Security ☐ Ambitions ☐ Personal Relations ☐ Sex Relations ☐ Pride/Shame ☐ Fear
Ask Ourselves: ** (AA 67.3) * (AA 62.2)	Putting out of our mind the wrong others had done, we resolutely looked for our own mistakes… We admitted our wrongs honestly…** **STEPS 4** and/or **10** - **(Column 4)**	
Where had I been selfish, self-centred or self-seeking?**		
Where had I been dishonest?**		
Where had I been frightened?**		
For what had I been responsible?**		
What decisions did I make based on self that later placed me in a position to be hurt?*		
When in the past did I make this decision? * (Earliest memory)		
Where was I wrong,** what was my part?		

STEPS 6 & 7 – List of Character Defects			

STEP 9 - Amends	STEP 8
	☐ Now ☐ Later ☐ Never

COLUMN WORK

Resentment (1) and/or Fear:	The Cause (Column 2)	Affects Our: (Column 3)
Person, Place or Thing		☐ Self-Esteem ☐ Security ☐ Ambitions ☐ Personal Relations ☐ Sex Relations ☐ Pride/Shame ☐ Fear
Ask Ourselves: ** (AA 67.3) * (AA 62.2)	Putting out of our mind the wrong others had done, we resolutely looked for our own mistakes… We admitted our wrongs honestly…** **STEPS 4** and/or **10** - **(Column 4)**	
Where had I been selfish, self-centred or self-seeking?**		
Where had I been dishonest?**		
Where had I been frightened?**		
For what had I been responsible?**		
What decisions did I make based on self that later placed me in a position to be hurt?*		
When in the past did I make this decision? * (Earliest memory)		
Where was I wrong,** what was my part?		

STEPS 6 & 7 – List of Character Defects					

STEP 9 - Amends	STEP 8
	☐ Now ☐ Later ☐ Never

FORMS ONLY

INVENTORY FORMS

Resentment (1) and/or Fear:	The Cause (Column 2)	Affects Our: (Column 3)
Person, Place or Thing		☐ Self-Esteem ☐ Security ☐ Ambitions ☐ Personal Relations ☐ Sex Relations ☐ Pride/Shame ☐ Fear
Ask Ourselves: ** (AA 67.3) * (AA 62.2)	Putting out of our mind the wrong others had done; we resolutely looked for our own mistakes... We admitted our wrongs honestly...** **STEPS 4** and/or **10 - (Column 4)**	
Where had I been selfish, self-centred or self-seeking?**		
Where had I been dishonest?**		
Where had I been frightened?**		
For what had I been responsible?**		
What decisions did I make based on self that later placed me in a position to be hurt?*		
When in the past did I make this decision? * (Earliest memory)		
Where was I wrong,** what was my part?		

STEPS 6 & 7 – List of Character Defects			

STEP 9 - Amends		STEP 8
		☐ Now ☐ Later ☐ Never

COLUMN WORK

Resentment (1) and/or Fear:	The Cause (Column 2)	Affects Our: (Column 3)
Person, Place or Thing		☐ Self-Esteem ☐ Security ☐ Ambitions ☐ Personal Relations ☐ Sex Relations ☐ Pride/Shame ☐ Fear
Ask Ourselves: ** (AA 67.3) * (AA 62.2)	Putting out of our mind the wrong others had done, we resolutely looked for our own mistakes… We admitted our wrongs honestly…** **STEPS 4** and/or **10** - **(Column 4)**	
Where had I been selfish, self-centred or self-seeking?**		
Where had I been dishonest?**		
Where had I been frightened?**		
For what had I been responsible?**		
What decisions did I make based on self that later placed me in a position to be hurt?*		
When in the past did I make this decision? * (Earliest memory)		
Where was I wrong,** what was my part?		

STEPS 6 & 7 – List of Character Defects				

STEP 9 - Amends	STEP 8
	☐ Now ☐ Later ☐ Never

FORMS ONLY

INVENTORY FORMS

Resentment (1) and/or Fear:	The Cause (Column 2)	Affects Our: (Column 3)
Person, Place or Thing		☐ Self-Esteem ☐ Security ☐ Ambitions ☐ Personal Relations ☐ Sex Relations ☐ Pride/Shame ☐ Fear
Ask Ourselves: ** (AA 67.3) * (AA 62.2)	Putting out of our mind the wrong others had done, we resolutely looked for our own mistakes... We admitted our wrongs honestly...** **STEPS 4** and/or **10 - (Column 4)**	
Where had I been selfish, self-centred or self-seeking?**		
Where had I been dishonest?**		
Where had I been frightened?**		
For what had I been responsible?**		
What decisions did I make based on self that later placed me in a position to be hurt?*		
When in the past did I make this decision? * (Earliest memory)		
Where was I wrong,** what was my part?		

STEPS 6 & 7 – List of Character Defects			

STEP 9 - Amends	STEP 8
	☐ **Now** ☐ **Later** ☐ **Never**

FOUR COLUMN INVENTORY...

COLUMN WORK

Resentment (1) and/or Fear:	The Cause (Column 2)	Affects Our: (Column 3)
Person, Place or Thing		☐ Self-Esteem ☐ Security ☐ Ambitions ☐ Personal Relations ☐ Sex Relations ☐ Pride/Shame ☐ Fear
Ask Ourselves: ** (AA 67.3) * (AA 62.2)	Putting out of our mind the wrong others had done, we resolutely looked for our own mistakes... We admitted our wrongs honestly...** STEPS 4 and/or 10 - (Column 4)	
Where had I been selfish, self-centred or self-seeking?**		
Where had I been dishonest?**		
Where had I been frightened?**		
For what had I been responsible?**		
What decisions did I make based on self that later placed me in a position to be hurt?*		
When in the past did I make this decision? * (Earliest memory)		
Where was I wrong,** what was my part?		

STEPS 6 & 7 – List of Character Defects

STEP 9 - Amends

	STEP 8
	☐ Now ☐ Later ☐ Never

FORMS ONLY

INVENTORY FORMS

Resentment (1) and/or Fear:	The Cause (Column 2)	Affects Our: (Column 3)
Person, Place or Thing		☐ Self-Esteem ☐ Security ☐ Ambitions ☐ Personal Relations ☐ Sex Relations ☐ Pride/Shame ☐ Fear
Ask Ourselves: ** (AA 67.3) * (AA 62.2)	Putting out of our mind the wrong others had done, we resolutely looked for our own mistakes... We admitted our wrongs honestly...** **STEPS 4 and/or 10 - (Column 4)**	
Where had I been selfish, self-centred or self-seeking?**		
Where had I been dishonest?**		
Where had I been frightened?**		
For what had I been responsible?**		
What decisions did I make based on self that later placed me in a position to be hurt?*		
When in the past did I make this decision? * (Earliest memory)		
Where was I wrong,** what was my part?		
STEPS 6 & 7 – List of Character Defects		
STEP 9 - Amends		**STEP 8**
		☐ Now ☐ Later ☐ Never

FOUR COLUMN INVENTORY...

COLUMN WORK

Resentment (1) and/or Fear:	The Cause (Column 2)	Affects Our: (Column 3)
Person, Place or Thing		☐ Self-Esteem ☐ Security ☐ Ambitions ☐ Personal Relations ☐ Sex Relations ☐ Pride/Shame ☐ Fear
Ask Ourselves: ** (AA 67.3) * (AA 62.2)	Putting out of our mind the wrong others had done, we resolutely looked for our own mistakes... We admitted our wrongs honestly... ** **STEPS 4 and/or 10 - (Column 4)**	
Where had I been selfish, self-centred or self-seeking?**		
Where had I been dishonest?**		
Where had I been frightened?**		
For what had I been responsible?**		
What decisions did I make based on self that later placed me in a position to be hurt?*		
When in the past did I make this decision? * (Earliest memory)		
Where was I wrong,** what was my part?		

STEPS 6 & 7 – List of Character Defects

STEP 9 - Amends	STEP 8
	☐ Now ☐ Later ☐ Never

FORMS ONLY

INVENTORY FORMS

Resentment (1) and/or Fear:	The Cause (Column 2)	Affects Our: (Column 3)
Person, Place or Thing		☐ Self-Esteem ☐ Security ☐ Ambitions ☐ Personal Relations ☐ Sex Relations ☐ Pride/Shame ☐ Fear
Ask Ourselves: ** (AA 67.3) * (AA 62.2)	Putting out of our mind the wrong others had done, we resolutely looked for our own mistakes... We admitted our wrongs honestly...** **STEPS 4** and/or **10** - **(Column 4)**	
Where had I been selfish, self-centred or self-seeking?**		
Where had I been dishonest?**		
Where had I been frightened?**		
For what had I been responsible?**		
What decisions did I make based on self that later placed me in a position to be hurt?*		
When in the past did I make this decision? * (Earliest memory)		
Where was I wrong,** what was my part?		
STEPS 6 & 7 – List of Character Defects		
STEP 9 - Amends		**STEP 8**
		☐ Now ☐ Later ☐ Never

COLUMN WORK

Resentment (1) and/or Fear:	The Cause (Column 2)	Affects Our: (Column 3)
Person, Place or Thing		☐ Self-Esteem ☐ Security ☐ Ambitions ☐ Personal Relations ☐ Sex Relations ☐ Pride/Shame ☐ Fear
Ask Ourselves: ** (AA 67.3) * (AA 62.2)	Putting out of our mind the wrong others had done, we resolutely looked for our own mistakes... We admitted our wrongs honestly...** **STEPS 4 and/or 10 - (Column 4)**	
Where had I been selfish, self-centred or self-seeking?**		
Where had I been dishonest?**		
Where had I been frightened?**		
For what had I been responsible?**		
What decisions did I make based on self that later placed me in a position to be hurt?*		
When in the past did I make this decision? * (Earliest memory)		
Where was I wrong,** what was my part?		
STEPS 6 & 7 – List of Character Defects		
STEP 9 - Amends		**STEP 8**
		☐ Now ☐ Later ☐ Never

INVENTORY FORMS

Resentment (1) and/or Fear:	The Cause (Column 2)	Affects Our: (Column 3)
Person, Place or Thing		☐ Self-Esteem ☐ Security ☐ Ambitions ☐ Personal Relations ☐ Sex Relations ☐ Pride/Shame ☐ Fear
Ask Ourselves: ** (AA 67.3) * (AA 62.2)	Putting out of our mind the wrong others had done, we resolutely looked for our own mistakes... We admitted our wrongs honestly...** **STEPS 4** and/or **10 - (Column 4)**	
Where had I been selfish, self-centred or self-seeking?**		
Where had I been dishonest?**		
Where had I been frightened?**		
For what had I been responsible?**		
What decisions did I make based on self that later placed me in a position to be hurt?*		
When in the past did I make this decision? * (Earliest memory)		
Where was I wrong,** what was my part?		

STEPS 6 & 7 – List of Character Defects				

STEP 9 - Amends	STEP 8
	☐ Now ☐ Later ☐ Never

FOUR COLUMN INVENTORY...

COLUMN WORK

Resentment (1) and/or Fear:	The Cause (Column 2)	Affects Our: (Column 3)
Person, Place or Thing		☐ Self-Esteem ☐ Security ☐ Ambitions ☐ Personal Relations ☐ Sex Relations ☐ Pride/Shame ☐ Fear
Ask Ourselves: ** (AA 67.3) * (AA 62.2)	Putting out of our mind the wrong others had done, we resolutely looked for our own mistakes... We admitted our wrongs honestly...** **STEPS 4** and/or **10** - **(Column 4)**	
Where had I been selfish, self-centred or self-seeking?**		
Where had I been dishonest?**		
Where had I been frightened?**		
For what had I been responsible?**		
What decisions did I make based on self that later placed me in a position to be hurt?*		
When in the past did I make this decision? * (Earliest memory)		
Where was I wrong,** what was my part?		
STEPS 6 & 7 – List of Character Defects		

STEP 9 - Amends	STEP 8
	☐ Now ☐ Later ☐ Never

FORMS ONLY

INVENTORY FORMS

Resentment (1) and/or Fear:	The Cause (Column 2)	Affects Our: (Column 3)
Person, Place or Thing		☐ Self-Esteem ☐ Security ☐ Ambitions ☐ Personal Relations ☐ Sex Relations ☐ Pride/Shame ☐ Fear
Ask Ourselves: ** (AA 67.3) * (AA 62.2)	Putting out of our mind the wrong others had done, we resolutely looked for our own mistakes... We admitted our wrongs honestly...** **STEPS 4 and/or 10 - (Column 4)**	
Where had I been selfish, self-centred or self-seeking?**		
Where had I been dishonest?**		
Where had I been frightened?**		
For what had I been responsible?**		
What decisions did I make based on self that later placed me in a position to be hurt?*		
When in the past did I make this decision? * (Earliest memory)		
Where was I wrong,** what was my part?		

STEPS 6 & 7 – List of Character Defects			

STEP 9 - Amends	STEP 8
	☐ Now ☐ Later ☐ Never

254 FOUR COLUMN INVENTORY...

COLUMN WORK

Resentment (1) and/or Fear:	The Cause (Column 2)	Affects Our: (Column 3)
Person, Place or Thing		☐ Self-Esteem ☐ Security ☐ Ambitions ☐ Personal Relations ☐ Sex Relations ☐ Pride/Shame ☐ Fear
Ask Ourselves: ** (AA 67.3) * (AA 62.2)	Putting out of our mind the wrong others had done, we resolutely looked for our own mistakes… We admitted our wrongs honestly…** **STEPS 4 and/or 10 - (Column 4)**	
Where had I been selfish, self-centred or self-seeking?**		
Where had I been dishonest?**		
Where had I been frightened?**		
For what had I been responsible?**		
What decisions did I make based on self that later placed me in a position to be hurt?*		
When in the past did I make this decision? * (Earliest memory)		
Where was I wrong,** what was my part?		

STEPS 6 & 7 – List of Character Defects				

STEP 9 - Amends	STEP 8
	☐ Now ☐ Later ☐ Never

FORMS ONLY

INVENTORY FORMS

Resentment (1) and/or Fear:	The Cause (Column 2)	Affects Our: (Column 3)
Person, Place or Thing		☐ Self-Esteem ☐ Security ☐ Ambitions ☐ Personal Relations ☐ Sex Relations ☐ Pride/Shame ☐ Fear
Ask Ourselves: ** (AA 67.3) * (AA 62.2)	Putting out of our mind the wrong others had done, we resolutely looked for our own mistakes... We admitted our wrongs honestly...** **STEPS 4** and/or **10 - (Column 4)**	
Where had I been selfish, self-centred or self-seeking?**		
Where had I been dishonest?**		
Where had I been frightened?**		
For what had I been responsible?**		
What decisions did I make based on self that later placed me in a position to be hurt?*		
When in the past did I make this decision? * (Earliest memory)		
Where was I wrong,** what was my part?		

STEPS 6 & 7 – List of Character Defects				

STEP 9 - Amends	STEP 8
	☐ Now ☐ Later ☐ Never

FOUR COLUMN INVENTORY...

COLUMN WORK

Resentment (1) and/or Fear:	The Cause (Column 2)	Affects Our: (Column 3)
Person, Place or Thing		☐ Self-Esteem ☐ Security ☐ Ambitions ☐ Personal Relations ☐ Sex Relations ☐ Pride/Shame ☐ Fear
Ask Ourselves: ** (AA 67.3) * (AA 62.2)	Putting out of our mind the wrong others had done, we resolutely looked for our own mistakes… We admitted our wrongs honestly…** STEPS 4 and/or **10 - (Column 4)**	
Where had I been selfish, self-centred or self-seeking?**		
Where had I been dishonest?**		
Where had I been frightened?**		
For what had I been responsible?**		
What decisions did I make based on self that later placed me in a position to be hurt?*		
When in the past did I make this decision? * (Earliest memory)		
Where was I wrong,** what was my part?		
STEPS 6 & 7 – List of Character Defects		
STEP 9 - Amends		**STEP 8**
		☐ Now ☐ Later ☐ Never

INVENTORY FORMS

Resentment (1) and/or Fear:	The Cause (Column 2)	Affects Our: (Column 3)
Person, Place or Thing		☐ Self-Esteem ☐ Security ☐ Ambitions ☐ Personal Relations ☐ Sex Relations ☐ Pride/Shame ☐ Fear
Ask Ourselves: ** (AA 67.3) * (AA 62.2)	Putting out of our mind the wrong others had done, we resolutely looked for our own mistakes... We admitted our wrongs honestly...** **STEPS 4 and/or 10 - (Column 4)**	
Where had I been selfish, self-centred or self-seeking?**		
Where had I been dishonest?**		
Where had I been frightened?**		
For what had I been responsible?**		
What decisions did I make based on self that later placed me in a position to be hurt?*		
When in the past did I make this decision? * (Earliest memory)		
Where was I wrong,** what was my part?		
STEPS 6 & 7 – List of Character Defects		
STEP 9 - Amends		**STEP 8**
		☐ Now ☐ Later ☐ Never

COLUMN WORK

Resentment (1) and/or Fear:	The Cause (Column 2)	Affects Our: (Column 3)
Person, Place or Thing		☐ Self-Esteem ☐ Security ☐ Ambitions ☐ Personal Relations ☐ Sex Relations ☐ Pride/Shame ☐ Fear
Ask Ourselves: ** (AA 67.3) * (AA 62.2)	Putting out of our mind the wrong others had done, we resolutely looked for our own mistakes… We admitted our wrongs honestly… ** **STEPS 4** and/or **10** - **(Column 4)**	
Where had I been selfish, self-centred or self-seeking?**		
Where had I been dishonest?**		
Where had I been frightened?**		
For what had I been responsible?**		
What decisions did I make based on self that later placed me in a position to be hurt?*		
When in the past did I make this decision? * (Earliest memory)		
Where was I wrong,** what was my part?		
STEPS 6 & 7 – List of Character Defects		

STEP 9 - Amends	STEP 8
	☐ Now ☐ Later ☐ Never

FORMS ONLY

INVENTORY FORMS

Resentment (1) and/or Fear:	The Cause (Column 2)	Affects Our: (Column 3)
Person, Place or Thing		☐ Self-Esteem ☐ Security ☐ Ambitions ☐ Personal Relations ☐ Sex Relations ☐ Pride/Shame ☐ Fear
Ask Ourselves: ** (AA 67.3) * (AA 62.2)	Putting out of our mind the wrong others had done, we resolutely looked for our own mistakes... We admitted our wrongs honestly...** **STEPS 4 and/or 10 - (Column 4)**	
Where had I been selfish, self-centred or self-seeking?**		
Where had I been dishonest?**		
Where had I been frightened?**		
For what had I been responsible?**		
What decisions did I make based on self that later placed me in a position to be hurt?*		
When in the past did I make this decision? * (Earliest memory)		
Where was I wrong,** what was my part?		
STEPS 6 & 7 – List of Character Defects		
STEP 9 - Amends		STEP 8
		☐ Now ☐ Later ☐ Never

260 FOUR COLUMN INVENTORY...

COLUMN WORK

Resentment and/or Fear: (1)	The Cause (Column 2)	Affects Our: (Column 3)
Person, Place or Thing		☐ Self-Esteem ☐ Security ☐ Ambitions ☐ Personal Relations ☐ Sex Relations ☐ Pride/Shame ☐ Fear
Ask Ourselves: ** (AA 67.3) * (AA 62.2)	Putting out of our mind the wrong others had done, we resolutely looked for our own mistakes... We admitted our wrongs honestly...** **STEPS 4** and/or **10** - **(Column 4)**	
Where had I been selfish, self-centred or self-seeking?**		
Where had I been dishonest?**		
Where had I been frightened?**		
For what had I been responsible?**		
What decisions did I make based on self that later placed me in a position to be hurt?*		
When in the past did I make this decision? * (Earliest memory)		
Where was I wrong,** what was my part?		

STEPS 6 & 7 – List of Character Defects			

STEP 9 - Amends	STEP 8
	☐ Now ☐ Later ☐ Never

FORMS ONLY

INVENTORY FORMS

Resentment (1) and/or Fear:	The Cause (Column 2)	Affects Our: (Column 3)
Person, Place or Thing		☐ Self-Esteem ☐ Security ☐ Ambitions ☐ Personal Relations ☐ Sex Relations ☐ Pride/Shame ☐ Fear
Ask Ourselves: ** (AA 67.3) * (AA 62.2)	Putting out of our mind the wrong others had done, we resolutely looked for our own mistakes... We admitted our wrongs honestly...** **STEPS 4** and/or **10 - (Column 4)**	
Where had I been selfish, self-centred or self-seeking?**		
Where had I been dishonest?**		
Where had I been frightened?**		
For what had I been responsible?**		
What decisions did I make based on self that later placed me in a position to be hurt?*		
When in the past did I make this decision? * (Earliest memory)		
Where was I wrong,** what was my part?		
STEPS 6 & 7 – List of Character Defects		
STEP 9 - Amends		**STEP 8**
		☐ Now ☐ Later ☐ Never

262 FOUR COLUMN INVENTORY...

COLUMN WORK

Resentment (1) and/or Fear:	The Cause (Column 2)	Affects Our: (Column 3)
Person, Place or Thing		☐ Self-Esteem ☐ Security ☐ Ambitions ☐ Personal Relations ☐ Sex Relations ☐ Pride/Shame ☐ Fear
Ask Ourselves: ** (AA 67.3) * (AA 62.2)	Putting out of our mind the wrong others had done, we resolutely looked for our own mistakes… We admitted our wrongs honestly…** **STEPS 4** and/or **10** - **(Column 4)**	
Where had I been selfish, self-centred or self-seeking?**		
Where had I been dishonest?**		
Where had I been frightened?**		
For what had I been responsible?**		
What decisions did I make based on self that later placed me in a position to be hurt?*		
When in the past did I make this decision? * (Earliest memory)		
Where was I wrong,** what was my part?		

STEPS 6 & 7 – List of Character Defects

STEP 9 - Amends	STEP 8
	☐ Now ☐ Later ☐ Never

FORMS ONLY

INVENTORY FORMS

Resentment (1) and/or Fear:	The Cause (Column 2)	Affects Our: (Column 3)
Person, Place or Thing		☐ Self-Esteem ☐ Security ☐ Ambitions ☐ Personal Relations ☐ Sex Relations ☐ Pride/Shame ☐ Fear
Ask Ourselves: ** (AA 67.3) * (AA 62.2)	Putting out of our mind the wrong others had done, we resolutely looked for our own mistakes... We admitted our wrongs honestly...** **STEPS 4 and/or 10 - (Column 4)**	
Where had I been selfish, self-centred or self-seeking?**		
Where had I been dishonest?**		
Where had I been frightened?**		
For what had I been responsible?**		
What decisions did I make based on self that later placed me in a position to be hurt?*		
When in the past did I make this decision? * (Earliest memory)		
Where was I wrong,** what was my part?		

STEPS 6 & 7 – List of Character Defects			

STEP 9 - Amends	STEP 8
	☐ Now ☐ Later ☐ Never

FOUR COLUMN INVENTORY...

COLUMN WORK

Resentment (1) and/or Fear:	The Cause (Column 2)	Affects Our: (Column 3)
Person, Place or Thing		☐ Self-Esteem ☐ Security ☐ Ambitions ☐ Personal Relations ☐ Sex Relations ☐ Pride/Shame ☐ Fear
Ask Ourselves: ** (AA 67.3) * (AA 62.2)	Putting out of our mind the wrong others had done, we resolutely looked for our own mistakes… We admitted our wrongs honestly…** **STEPS 4** and/or **10** - **(Column 4)**	
Where had I been selfish, self-centred or self-seeking?**		
Where had I been dishonest?**		
Where had I been frightened?**		
For what had I been responsible?**		
What decisions did I make based on self that later placed me in a position to be hurt?*		
When in the past did I make this decision? * (Earliest memory)		
Where was I wrong,** what was my part?		

STEPS 6 & 7 – List of Character Defects				

STEP 9 - Amends	STEP 8
	☐ Now ☐ Later ☐ Never

FORMS ONLY

INVENTORY FORMS

Resentment (1) and/or Fear:	The Cause (Column 2)	Affects Our: (Column 3)
Person, Place or Thing		☐ Self-Esteem ☐ Security ☐ Ambitions ☐ Personal Relations ☐ Sex Relations ☐ Pride/Shame ☐ Fear
Ask Ourselves: ** (AA 67.3) * (AA 62.2)	Putting out of our mind the wrong others had done, we resolutely looked for our own mistakes… We admitted our wrongs honestly…** **STEPS 4** and/or **10 - (Column 4)**	
Where had I been selfish, self-centred or self-seeking?**		
Where had I been dishonest?**		
Where had I been frightened?**		
For what had I been responsible?**		
What decisions did I make based on self that later placed me in a position to be hurt?*		
When in the past did I make this decision? * (Earliest memory)		
Where was I wrong,** what was my part?		

STEPS 6 & 7 – List of Character Defects			

STEP 9 - Amends	STEP 8
	☐ Now ☐ Later ☐ Never

COLUMN WORK

Resentment (1) and/or Fear:	The Cause (Column 2)	Affects Our: (Column 3)
Person, Place or Thing		☐ Self-Esteem ☐ Security ☐ Ambitions ☐ Personal Relations ☐ Sex Relations ☐ Pride/Shame ☐ Fear
Ask Ourselves: ** (AA 67.3) * (AA 62.2)	Putting out of our mind the wrong others had done, we resolutely looked for our own mistakes... We admitted our wrongs honestly...** **STEPS 4 and/or 10 - (Column 4)**	
Where had I been selfish, self-centred or self-seeking?**		
Where had I been dishonest?**		
Where had I been frightened?**		
For what had I been responsible?**		
What decisions did I make based on self that later placed me in a position to be hurt?*		
When in the past did I make this decision? * (Earliest memory)		
Where was I wrong,** what was my part?		

STEPS 6 & 7 – List of Character Defects					

STEP 9 - Amends	STEP 8
	☐ Now ☐ Later ☐ Never

FORMS ONLY

INVENTORY FORMS

Resentment (1) and/or Fear:	The Cause (Column 2)	Affects Our: (Column 3)
Person, Place or Thing		☐ Self-Esteem ☐ Security ☐ Ambitions ☐ Personal Relations ☐ Sex Relations ☐ Pride/Shame ☐ Fear
Ask Ourselves: ** (AA 67.3) * (AA 62.2)	Putting out of our mind the wrong others had done, we resolutely looked for our own mistakes… We admitted our wrongs honestly…** **STEPS 4** and/or **10 - (Column 4)**	
Where had I been selfish, self-centred or self-seeking?**		
Where had I been dishonest?**		
Where had I been frightened?**		
For what had I been responsible?**		
What decisions did I make based on self that later placed me in a position to be hurt?*		
When in the past did I make this decision? * (Earliest memory)		
Where was I wrong,** what was my part?		

STEPS 6 & 7 – List of Character Defects			

STEP 9 - Amends	STEP 8
	☐ Now ☐ Later ☐ Never

268   FOUR COLUMN INVENTORY…

COLUMN WORK

Resentment and/or Fear: (1)	The Cause (Column 2)	Affects Our: (Column 3)
Person, Place or Thing		☐ Self-Esteem ☐ Security ☐ Ambitions ☐ Personal Relations ☐ Sex Relations ☐ Pride/Shame ☐ Fear
Ask Ourselves: ** (AA 67.3) * (AA 62.2)	Putting out of our mind the wrong others had done, we resolutely looked for our own mistakes… We admitted our wrongs honestly…** **STEPS 4** and/or **10** - **(Column 4)**	
Where had I been selfish, self-centred or self-seeking?**		
Where had I been dishonest?**		
Where had I been frightened?**		
For what had I been responsible?**		
What decisions did I make based on self that later placed me in a position to be hurt?*		
When in the past did I make this decision? * (Earliest memory)		
Where was I wrong,** what was my part?		

STEPS 6 & 7 – List of Character Defects

STEP 9 - Amends	STEP 8
	☐ Now ☐ Later ☐ Never

FORMS ONLY

INVENTORY FORMS

Resentment (1) and/or Fear:	The Cause (Column 2)	Affects Our: (Column 3)
Person, Place or Thing		☐ Self-Esteem ☐ Security ☐ Ambitions ☐ Personal Relations ☐ Sex Relations ☐ Pride/Shame ☐ Fear
Ask Ourselves: ** (AA 67.3) * (AA 62.2)	Putting out of our mind the wrong others had done, we resolutely looked for our own mistakes... We admitted our wrongs honestly...** **STEPS 4 and/or 10 - (Column 4)**	
Where had I been selfish, self-centred or self-seeking?**		
Where had I been dishonest?**		
Where had I been frightened?**		
For what had I been responsible?**		
What decisions did I make based on self that later placed me in a position to be hurt?*		
When in the past did I make this decision? * (Earliest memory)		
Where was I wrong,** what was my part?		

STEPS 6 & 7 – List of Character Defects

STEP 9 - Amends	STEP 8
	☐ Now ☐ Later ☐ Never

FOUR COLUMN INVENTORY...

COLUMN WORK

Resentment (1) and/or Fear:	The Cause (Column 2)	Affects Our: (Column 3)
Person, Place or Thing		☐ Self-Esteem ☐ Security ☐ Ambitions ☐ Personal Relations ☐ Sex Relations ☐ Pride/Shame ☐ Fear
Ask Ourselves: ** (AA 67.3) * (AA 62.2)	Putting out of our mind the wrong others had done, we resolutely looked for our own mistakes... We admitted our wrongs honestly...** **STEPS 4** and/or **10** - **(Column 4)**	
Where had I been selfish, self-centred or self-seeking?**		
Where had I been dishonest?**		
Where had I been frightened?**		
For what had I been responsible?**		
What decisions did I make based on self that later placed me in a position to be hurt?*		
When in the past did I make this decision? * (Earliest memory)		
Where was I wrong,** what was my part?		

STEPS 6 & 7 – List of Character Defects

STEP 9 - Amends	STEP 8
	☐ Now ☐ Later ☐ Never

INVENTORY FORMS

Resentment (1) and/or Fear:	The Cause (Column 2)	Affects Our: (Column 3)
Person, Place or Thing		☐ Self-Esteem ☐ Security ☐ Ambitions ☐ Personal Relations ☐ Sex Relations ☐ Pride/Shame ☐ Fear
Ask Ourselves: ** (AA 67.3) * (AA 62.2)	Putting out of our mind the wrong others had done, we resolutely looked for our own mistakes... We admitted our wrongs honestly...** **STEPS 4** and/or **10 - (Column 4)**	
Where had I been selfish, self-centred or self-seeking?**		
Where had I been dishonest?**		
Where had I been frightened?**		
For what had I been responsible?**		
What decisions did I make based on self that later placed me in a position to be hurt?*		
When in the past did I make this decision? * (Earliest memory)		
Where was I wrong,** what was my part?		
STEPS 6 & 7 – List of Character Defects				
STEP 9 - Amends			**STEP 8**
			☐ Now ☐ Later ☐ Never

COLUMN WORK

Resentment and/or Fear: (1)	The Cause (Column 2)	Affects Our: (Column 3)
Person, Place or Thing		☐ Self-Esteem ☐ Security ☐ Ambitions ☐ Personal Relations ☐ Sex Relations ☐ Pride/Shame ☐ Fear
Ask Ourselves: ** (AA 67.3) * (AA 62.2)	Putting out of our mind the wrong others had done, we resolutely looked for our own mistakes… We admitted our wrongs honestly…** **STEPS 4** and/or **10 - (Column 4)**	
Where had I been selfish, self-centred or self-seeking?**		
Where had I been dishonest?**		
Where had I been frightened?**		
For what had I been responsible?**		
What decisions did I make based on self that later placed me in a position to be hurt?*		
When in the past did I make this decision? * (Earliest memory)		
Where was I wrong,** what was my part?		

STEPS 6 & 7 – List of Character Defects				

STEP 9 - Amends	STEP 8
	☐ Now ☐ Later ☐ Never

FORMS ONLY

INVENTORY FORMS

Resentment (1) and/or Fear:	The Cause (Column 2)	Affects Our: (Column 3)
Person, Place or Thing		☐ Self-Esteem ☐ Security ☐ Ambitions ☐ Personal Relations ☐ Sex Relations ☐ Pride/Shame ☐ Fear
Ask Ourselves: ** (AA 67.3) * (AA 62.2)	Putting out of our mind the wrong others had done, we resolutely looked for our own mistakes… We admitted our wrongs honestly…** **STEPS 4** and/or **10** - **(Column 4)**	
Where had I been selfish, self-centred or self-seeking?**		
Where had I been dishonest?**		
Where had I been frightened?**		
For what had I been responsible?**		
What decisions did I make based on self that later placed me in a position to be hurt?*		
When in the past did I make this decision? * (Earliest memory)		
Where was I wrong,** what was my part?		

STEPS 6 & 7 – List of Character Defects

STEP 9 - Amends	STEP 8
	☐ Now ☐ Later ☐ Never

FOUR COLUMN INVENTORY…

COLUMN WORK

Resentment (1) and/or Fear:	The Cause (Column 2)	Affects Our: (Column 3)
Person, Place or Thing		☐ Self-Esteem ☐ Security ☐ Ambitions ☐ Personal Relations ☐ Sex Relations ☐ Pride/Shame ☐ Fear
Ask Ourselves: ** (AA 67.3) * (AA 62.2)	Putting out of our mind the wrong others had done, we resolutely looked for our own mistakes… We admitted our wrongs honestly…** **STEPS 4** and/or **10 - (Column 4)**	
Where had I been selfish, self-centred or self-seeking?**		
Where had I been dishonest?**		
Where had I been frightened?**		
For what had I been responsible?**		
What decisions did I make based on self that later placed me in a position to be hurt?*		
When in the past did I make this decision? * (Earliest memory)		
Where was I wrong,** what was my part?		

STEPS 6 & 7 – List of Character Defects				

STEP 9 - Amends	STEP 8
	☐ Now ☐ Later ☐ Never

FORMS ONLY

INVENTORY FORMS

Resentment (1) and/or Fear:	The Cause (Column 2)	Affects Our: (Column 3)
Person, Place or Thing		☐ Self-Esteem ☐ Security ☐ Ambitions ☐ Personal Relations ☐ Sex Relations ☐ Pride/Shame ☐ Fear
Ask Ourselves: ** (AA 67.3) * (AA 62.2)	Putting out of our mind the wrong others had done, we resolutely looked for our own mistakes... We admitted our wrongs honestly...** **STEPS 4** and/or **10 - (Column 4)**	
Where had I been selfish, self-centred or self-seeking?**		
Where had I been dishonest?**		
Where had I been frightened?**		
For what had I been responsible?**		
What decisions did I make based on self that later placed me in a position to be hurt?*		
When in the past did I make this decision? * (Earliest memory)		
Where was I wrong,** what was my part?		

STEPS 6 & 7 – List of Character Defects			

STEP 9 - Amends	STEP 8
	☐ Now ☐ Later ☐ Never

FOUR COLUMN INVENTORY...

COLUMN WORK

Resentment (1) and/or Fear:	The Cause (Column 2)	Affects Our: (Column 3)
Person, Place or Thing		☐ Self-Esteem ☐ Security ☐ Ambitions ☐ Personal Relations ☐ Sex Relations ☐ Pride/Shame ☐ Fear
Ask Ourselves: ** (AA 67.3) * (AA 62.2)	Putting out of our mind the wrong others had done, we resolutely looked for our own mistakes... We admitted our wrongs honestly...** **STEPS 4 and/or 10 - (Column 4)**	
Where had I been selfish, self-centred or self-seeking?**		
Where had I been dishonest?**		
Where had I been frightened?**		
For what had I been responsible?**		
What decisions did I make based on self that later placed me in a position to be hurt?*		
When in the past did I make this decision? * (Earliest memory)		
Where was I wrong,** what was my part?		

STEPS 6 & 7 – List of Character Defects			

STEP 9 - Amends	STEP 8
	☐ Now ☐ Later ☐ Never

INVENTORY FORMS

Resentment (1) and/or Fear:	The Cause (Column 2)	Affects Our: (Column 3)
Person, Place or Thing		☐ Self-Esteem ☐ Security ☐ Ambitions ☐ Personal Relations ☐ Sex Relations ☐ Pride/Shame ☐ Fear
Ask Ourselves: ** (AA 67.3) * (AA 62.2)	Putting out of our mind the wrong others had done, we resolutely looked for our own mistakes... We admitted our wrongs honestly...** **STEPS 4** and/or **10** - **(Column 4)**	
Where had I been selfish, self-centred or self-seeking?**		
Where had I been dishonest?**		
Where had I been frightened?**		
For what had I been responsible?**		
What decisions did I make based on self that later placed me in a position to be hurt?*		
When in the past did I make this decision? * (Earliest memory)		
Where was I wrong,** what was my part?		
STEPS 6 & 7 – List of Character Defects		
STEP 9 - Amends		**STEP 8**
		☐ Now ☐ Later ☐ Never

FOUR COLUMN INVENTORY...

COLUMN WORK

Resentment and/or Fear: (1)	The Cause (Column 2)	Affects Our: (Column 3)
Person, Place or Thing		☐ Self-Esteem ☐ Security ☐ Ambitions ☐ Personal Relations ☐ Sex Relations ☐ Pride/Shame ☐ Fear
Ask Ourselves: ** (AA 67.3) * (AA 62.2)	Putting out of our mind the wrong others had done, we resolutely looked for our own mistakes… We admitted our wrongs honestly…** **STEPS 4 and/or 10 - (Column 4)**	
Where had I been selfish, self-centred or self-seeking?**		
Where had I been dishonest?**		
Where had I been frightened?**		
For what had I been responsible?**		
What decisions did I make based on self that later placed me in a position to be hurt?*		
When in the past did I make this decision? * (Earliest memory)		
Where was I wrong,** what was my part?		

STEPS 6 & 7 – List of Character Defects

STEP 9 - Amends	STEP 8
	☐ Now ☐ Later ☐ Never

FORMS ONLY

INVENTORY FORMS

Resentment (1) and/or Fear:	The Cause (Column 2)	Affects Our: (Column 3)
Person, Place or Thing		☐ Self-Esteem ☐ Security ☐ Ambitions ☐ Personal Relations ☐ Sex Relations ☐ Pride/Shame ☐ Fear
Ask Ourselves: ** (AA 67.3) * (AA 62.2)	Putting out of our mind the wrong others had done, we resolutely looked for our own mistakes... We admitted our wrongs honestly...** **STEPS 4** and/or **10** - **(Column 4)**	
Where had I been selfish, self-centred or self-seeking?**		
Where had I been dishonest?**		
Where had I been frightened?**		
For what had I been responsible?**		
What decisions did I make based on self that later placed me in a position to be hurt?*		
When in the past did I make this decision? * (Earliest memory)		
Where was I wrong,** what was my part?		
STEPS 6 & 7 – List of Character Defects		
STEP 9 - Amends		STEP 8
		☐ Now ☐ Later ☐ Never

FOUR COLUMN INVENTORY...

COLUMN WORK

Resentment and/or Fear: (1)	The Cause (Column 2)	Affects Our: (Column 3)
Person, Place or Thing		☐ Self-Esteem ☐ Security ☐ Ambitions ☐ Personal Relations ☐ Sex Relations ☐ Pride/Shame ☐ Fear
Ask Ourselves: ** (AA 67.3) * (AA 62.2)	Putting out of our mind the wrong others had done, we resolutely looked for our own mistakes... We admitted our wrongs honestly... ** **STEPS 4** and/or **10** - **(Column 4)**	
Where had I been selfish, self-centred or self-seeking?**		
Where had I been dishonest?**		
Where had I been frightened?**		
For what had I been responsible?**		
What decisions did I make based on self that later placed me in a position to be hurt?*		
When in the past did I make this decision? * (Earliest memory)		
Where was I wrong,** what was my part?		

STEPS 6 & 7 – List of Character Defects

STEP 9 – Amends

	STEP 8
	☐ Now ☐ Later ☐ Never

FORMS ONLY

INVENTORY FORMS

Resentment (1) and/or Fear:	The Cause (Column 2)	Affects Our: (Column 3)
Person, Place or Thing		☐ Self-Esteem ☐ Security ☐ Ambitions ☐ Personal Relations ☐ Sex Relations ☐ Pride/Shame ☐ Fear
Ask Ourselves: ** (AA 67.3) * (AA 62.2)	Putting out of our mind the wrong others had done, we resolutely looked for our own mistakes... We admitted our wrongs honestly... ** **STEPS 4** and/or **10 - (Column 4)**	
Where had I been selfish, self-centred or self-seeking?**		
Where had I been dishonest?**		
Where had I been frightened?**		
For what had I been responsible?**		
What decisions did I make based on self that later placed me in a position to be hurt?*		
When in the past did I make this decision? * (Earliest memory)		
Where was I wrong,** what was my part?		
STEPS 6 & 7 – List of Character Defects		
STEP 9 - Amends		**STEP 8**
		☐ Now ☐ Later ☐ Never

COLUMN WORK

Resentment (1) and/or Fear:	The Cause (Column 2)	Affects Our: (Column 3)
Person, Place or Thing		☐ Self-Esteem ☐ Security ☐ Ambitions ☐ Personal Relations ☐ Sex Relations ☐ Pride/Shame ☐ Fear
Ask Ourselves: ** (AA 67.3) * (AA 62.2)	Putting out of our mind the wrong others had done, we resolutely looked for our own mistakes… We admitted our wrongs honestly…** **STEPS 4 and/or 10 – (Column 4)**	
Where had I been selfish, self-centred or self-seeking?**		
Where had I been dishonest?**		
Where had I been frightened?**		
For what had I been responsible?**		
What decisions did I make based on self that later placed me in a position to be hurt?*		
When in the past did I make this decision? * (Earliest memory)		
Where was I wrong,** what was my part?		

STEPS 6 & 7 – List of Character Defects

STEP 9 – Amends	STEP 8
	☐ Now ☐ Later ☐ Never

INVENTORY FORMS

Resentment (1) and/or Fear:	The Cause (Column 2)	Affects Our: (Column 3)
Person, Place or Thing		☐ Self-Esteem ☐ Security ☐ Ambitions ☐ Personal Relations ☐ Sex Relations ☐ Pride/Shame ☐ Fear
Ask Ourselves: ** (AA 67.3) * (AA 62.2)	Putting out of our mind the wrong others had done, we resolutely looked for our own mistakes… We admitted our wrongs honestly…** **STEPS 4** and/or **10** - **(Column 4)**	
Where had I been selfish, self-centred or self-seeking?**		
Where had I been dishonest?**		
Where had I been frightened?**		
For what had I been responsible?**		
What decisions did I make based on self that later placed me in a position to be hurt?*		
When in the past did I make this decision? * (Earliest memory)		
Where was I wrong,** what was my part?		

STEPS 6 & 7 – List of Character Defects			

STEP 9 - Amends	STEP 8
	☐ Now ☐ Later ☐ Never

COLUMN WORK

Resentment (1) and/or Fear:	The Cause (Column 2)	Affects Our: (Column 3)
Person, Place or Thing		☐ Self-Esteem ☐ Security ☐ Ambitions ☐ Personal Relations ☐ Sex Relations ☐ Pride/Shame ☐ Fear
Ask Ourselves: ** (AA 67.3) * (AA 62.2)	Putting out of our mind the wrong others had done, we resolutely looked for our own mistakes… We admitted our wrongs honestly…** **STEPS 4 and/or 10 - (Column 4)**	
Where had I been selfish, self-centred or self-seeking?**		
Where had I been dishonest?**		
Where had I been frightened?**		
For what had I been responsible?**		
What decisions did I make based on self that later placed me in a position to be hurt?*		
When in the past did I make this decision? * (Earliest memory)		
Where was I wrong,** what was my part?		

STEPS 6 & 7 – List of Character Defects				

STEP 9 - Amends	STEP 8
	☐ Now ☐ Later ☐ Never

FORMS ONLY

INVENTORY FORMS

Resentment (1) and/or Fear:	The Cause (Column 2)	Affects Our: (Column 3)
Person, Place or Thing		☐ Self-Esteem ☐ Security ☐ Ambitions ☐ Personal Relations ☐ Sex Relations ☐ Pride/Shame ☐ Fear
Ask Ourselves: ** (AA 67.3) * (AA 62.2)	Putting out of our mind the wrong others had done, we resolutely looked for our own mistakes... We admitted our wrongs honestly...** **STEPS 4 and/or 10 - (Column 4)**	
Where had I been selfish, self-centred or self-seeking?**		
Where had I been dishonest?**		
Where had I been frightened?**		
For what had I been responsible?**		
What decisions did I make based on self that later placed me in a position to be hurt?*		
When in the past did I make this decision? * (Earliest memory)		
Where was I wrong,** what was my part?		

STEPS 6 & 7 – List of Character Defects			

STEP 9 - Amends	STEP 8
	☐ Now ☐ Later ☐ Never

286   FOUR COLUMN INVENTORY...

COLUMN WORK

Resentment and/or Fear: (1)	The Cause (Column 2)	Affects Our: (Column 3)
Person, Place or Thing		☐ Self-Esteem ☐ Security ☐ Ambitions ☐ Personal Relations ☐ Sex Relations ☐ Pride/Shame ☐ Fear
Ask Ourselves: ** (AA 67.3) * (AA 62.2)	Putting out of our mind the wrong others had done, we resolutely looked for our own mistakes... We admitted our wrongs honestly...** **STEPS 4** and/or **10** - **(Column 4)**	
Where had I been selfish, self-centred or self-seeking?**		
Where had I been dishonest?**		
Where had I been frightened?**		
For what had I been responsible?**		
What decisions did I make based on self that later placed me in a position to be hurt?*		
When in the past did I make this decision? * (Earliest memory)		
Where was I wrong,** what was my part?		
STEPS 6 & 7 – List of Character Defects		

STEP 9 - Amends		STEP 8
		☐ Now ☐ Later ☐ Never

FORMS ONLY

INVENTORY FORMS

Resentment (1) and/or Fear:	The Cause (Column 2)	Affects Our: (Column 3)
Person, Place or Thing		☐ Self-Esteem ☐ Security ☐ Ambitions ☐ Personal Relations ☐ Sex Relations ☐ Pride/Shame ☐ Fear
Ask Ourselves: ** (AA 67.3) * (AA 62.2)	Putting out of our mind the wrong others had done, we resolutely looked for our own mistakes... We admitted our wrongs honestly...** **STEPS 4** and/or **10 - (Column 4)**	
Where had I been selfish, self-centred or self-seeking?**		
Where had I been dishonest?**		
Where had I been frightened?**		
For what had I been responsible?**		
What decisions did I make based on self that later placed me in a position to be hurt?*		
When in the past did I make this decision? * (Earliest memory)		
Where was I wrong,** what was my part?		
STEPS 6 & 7 – List of Character Defects		
STEP 9 - Amends		**STEP 8**
		☐ Now ☐ Later ☐ Never

FOUR COLUMN INVENTORY...

COLUMN WORK

Resentment (1) and/or Fear:	The Cause (Column 2)	Affects Our: (Column 3)
Person, Place or Thing		☐ Self-Esteem ☐ Security ☐ Ambitions ☐ Personal Relations ☐ Sex Relations ☐ Pride/Shame ☐ Fear
Ask Ourselves: ** (AA 67.3) * (AA 62.2)	Putting out of our mind the wrong others had done, we resolutely looked for our own mistakes... We admitted our wrongs honestly...** **STEPS 4** and/or **10** - **(Column 4)**	
Where had I been selfish, self-centred or self-seeking?**		
Where had I been dishonest?**		
Where had I been frightened?**		
For what had I been responsible?**		
What decisions did I make based on self that later placed me in a position to be hurt?*		
When in the past did I make this decision? * (Earliest memory)		
Where was I wrong,** what was my part?		
STEPS 6 & 7 – List of Character Defects				
---	---	---	---	---

STEP 9 - Amends	STEP 8
	☐ Now ☐ Later ☐ Never

FORMS ONLY

INVENTORY FORMS

Resentment (1) and/or Fear:	The Cause (Column 2)	Affects Our: (Column 3)
Person, Place or Thing		☐ Self-Esteem ☐ Security ☐ Ambitions ☐ Personal Relations ☐ Sex Relations ☐ Pride/Shame ☐ Fear
Ask Ourselves: ** (AA 67.3) * (AA 62.2)	Putting out of our mind the wrong others had done, we resolutely looked for our own mistakes... We admitted our wrongs honestly...** **STEPS 4** and/or **10 - (Column 4)**	
Where had I been selfish, self-centred or self-seeking?**		
Where had I been dishonest?**		
Where had I been frightened?**		
For what had I been responsible?**		
What decisions did I make based on self that later placed me in a position to be hurt?*		
When in the past did I make this decision? * (Earliest memory)		
Where was I wrong,** what was my part?		
STEPS 6 & 7 – List of Character Defects		
STEP 9 - Amends		**STEP 8**
		☐ Now ☐ Later ☐ Never

FOUR COLUMN INVENTORY...

COLUMN WORK

Resentment (1) and/or Fear:	The Cause (Column 2)	Affects Our: (Column 3)
Person, Place or Thing		☐ Self-Esteem ☐ Security ☐ Ambitions ☐ Personal Relations ☐ Sex Relations ☐ Pride/Shame ☐ Fear
Ask Ourselves: ** (AA 67.3) * (AA 62.2)	Putting out of our mind the wrong others had done, we resolutely looked for our own mistakes... We admitted our wrongs honestly...** **STEPS 4 and/or 10 - (Column 4)**	
Where had I been selfish, self-centred or self-seeking?**		
Where had I been dishonest?**		
Where had I been frightened?**		
For what had I been responsible?**		
What decisions did I make based on self that later placed me in a position to be hurt?*		
When in the past did I make this decision? * (Earliest memory)		
Where was I wrong,** what was my part?		

STEPS 6 & 7 – List of Character Defects

STEP 9 - Amends	**STEP 8**
	☐ Now ☐ Later ☐ Never

INVENTORY FORMS

Resentment (1) and/or Fear:	The Cause (Column 2)	Affects Our: (Column 3)
Person, Place or Thing		☐ Self-Esteem ☐ Security ☐ Ambitions ☐ Personal Relations ☐ Sex Relations ☐ Pride/Shame ☐ Fear
Ask Ourselves: ** (AA 67.3) * (AA 62.2)	Putting out of our mind the wrong others had done, we resolutely looked for our own mistakes... We admitted our wrongs honestly...** **STEPS 4** and/or **10 - (Column 4)**	
Where had I been selfish, self-centred or self-seeking?**		
Where had I been dishonest?**		
Where had I been frightened?**		
For what had I been responsible?**		
What decisions did I make based on self that later placed me in a position to be hurt?*		
When in the past did I make this decision? * (Earliest memory)		
Where was I wrong,** what was my part?		
STEPS 6 & 7 – List of Character Defects			
STEP 9 - Amends		**STEP 8**
		☐ Now ☐ Later ☐ Never

FOUR COLUMN INVENTORY...

COLUMN WORK

Resentment (1) and/or Fear:	The Cause (Column 2)	Affects Our: (Column 3)
Person, Place or Thing		☐ Self-Esteem ☐ Security ☐ Ambitions ☐ Personal Relations ☐ Sex Relations ☐ Pride/Shame ☐ Fear
Ask Ourselves: ** (AA 67.3) * (AA 62.2)	Putting out of our mind the wrong others had done, we resolutely looked for our own mistakes… We admitted our wrongs honestly…** **STEPS 4** and/or **10** - (Column 4)	
Where had I been selfish, self-centred or self-seeking?**		
Where had I been dishonest?**		
Where had I been frightened?**		
For what had I been responsible?**		
What decisions did I make based on self that later placed me in a position to be hurt?*		
When in the past did I make this decision? * (Earliest memory)		
Where was I wrong,** what was my part?		

STEPS 6 & 7 – List of Character Defects				

STEP 9 - Amends	STEP 8
	☐ Now ☐ Later ☐ Never

FORMS ONLY

INVENTORY FORMS

Resentment (1) and/or Fear:	The Cause (Column 2)	Affects Our: (Column 3)
Person, Place or Thing		☐ Self-Esteem ☐ Security ☐ Ambitions ☐ Personal Relations ☐ Sex Relations ☐ Pride/Shame ☐ Fear
Ask Ourselves: ** (AA 67.3) * (AA 62.2)	Putting out of our mind the wrong others had done, we resolutely looked for our own mistakes... We admitted our wrongs honestly...** **STEPS 4 and/or 10 - (Column 4)**	
Where had I been selfish, self-centred or self-seeking?**		
Where had I been dishonest?**		
Where had I been frightened?**		
For what had I been responsible?**		
What decisions did I make based on self that later placed me in a position to be hurt?*		
When in the past did I make this decision? * (Earliest memory)		
Where was I wrong,** what was my part?		
STEPS 6 & 7 – List of Character Defects		
STEP 9 - Amends		STEP 8
		☐ Now ☐ Later ☐ Never

COLUMN WORK

Resentment and/or Fear: (1)	The Cause (Column 2)	Affects Our: (Column 3)
Person, Place or Thing		☐ Self-Esteem ☐ Security ☐ Ambitions ☐ Personal Relations ☐ Sex Relations ☐ Pride/Shame ☐ Fear
Ask Ourselves: ** (AA 67.3) * (AA 62.2)	Putting out of our mind the wrong others had done, we resolutely looked for our own mistakes... We admitted our wrongs honestly...** **STEPS 4 and/or 10 - (Column 4)**	
Where had I been selfish, self-centred or self-seeking?**		
Where had I been dishonest?**		
Where had I been frightened?**		
For what had I been responsible?**		
What decisions did I make based on self that later placed me in a position to be hurt?*		
When in the past did I make this decision? * (Earliest memory)		
Where was I wrong,** what was my part?		

STEPS 6 & 7 – List of Character Defects			

STEP 9 - Amends	STEP 8
	☐ Now ☐ Later ☐ Never

FORMS ONLY

INVENTORY FORMS

Resentment (1) and/or Fear:	The Cause (Column 2)	Affects Our: (Column 3)
Person, Place or Thing		☐ Self-Esteem ☐ Security ☐ Ambitions ☐ Personal Relations ☐ Sex Relations ☐ Pride/Shame ☐ Fear
Ask Ourselves: ** (AA 67.3) * (AA 62.2)	Putting out of our mind the wrong others had done, we resolutely looked for our own mistakes… We admitted our wrongs honestly…** **STEPS 4** and/or **10** - **(Column 4)**	
Where had I been selfish, self-centred or self-seeking?**		
Where had I been dishonest?**		
Where had I been frightened?**		
For what had I been responsible?**		
What decisions did I make based on self that later placed me in a position to be hurt?*		
When in the past did I make this decision? * (Earliest memory)		
Where was I wrong,** what was my part?		

STEPS 6 & 7 – List of Character Defects			

STEP 9 - Amends	STEP 8
	☐ Now ☐ Later ☐ Never

COLUMN WORK

Resentment (1) and/or Fear:	The Cause (Column 2)	Affects Our: (Column 3)
Person, Place or Thing		☐ Self-Esteem ☐ Security ☐ Ambitions ☐ Personal Relations ☐ Sex Relations ☐ Pride/Shame ☐ Fear
Ask Ourselves: ** (AA 67.3) * (AA 62.2)	Putting out of our mind the wrong others had done, we resolutely looked for our own mistakes... We admitted our wrongs honestly... ** STEPS 4 and/or 10 - (Column 4)	
Where had I been selfish, self-centred or self-seeking?**		
Where had I been dishonest?**		
Where had I been frightened?**		
For what had I been responsible?**		
What decisions did I make based on self that later placed me in a position to be hurt?*		
When in the past did I make this decision? * (Earliest memory)		
Where was I wrong,** what was my part?		

STEPS 6 & 7 – List of Character Defects				

STEP 9 - Amends	STEP 8
	☐ Now ☐ Later ☐ Never

INVENTORY FORMS

Resentment (1) and/or Fear:	The Cause (Column 2)	Affects Our: (Column 3)
Person, Place or Thing		☐ Self-Esteem ☐ Security ☐ Ambitions ☐ Personal Relations ☐ Sex Relations ☐ Pride/Shame ☐ Fear
Ask Ourselves: ** (AA 67.3) * (AA 62.2)	Putting out of our mind the wrong others had done, we resolutely looked for our own mistakes... We admitted our wrongs honestly...** **STEPS 4** and/or **10 - (Column 4)**	
Where had I been selfish, self-centred or self-seeking?**		
Where had I been dishonest?**		
Where had I been frightened?**		
For what had I been responsible?**		
What decisions did I make based on self that later placed me in a position to be hurt?*		
When in the past did I make this decision? * (Earliest memory)		
Where was I wrong,** what was my part?		

STEPS 6 & 7 – List of Character Defects			

STEP 9 - Amends	STEP 8
	☐ Now ☐ Later ☐ Never

COLUMN WORK

Resentment and/or Fear: (1)	The Cause (Column 2)	Affects Our: (Column 3)
Person, Place or Thing		☐ Self-Esteem ☐ Security ☐ Ambitions ☐ Personal Relations ☐ Sex Relations ☐ Pride/Shame ☐ Fear
Ask Ourselves: ** (AA 67.3) * (AA 62.2)	Putting out of our mind the wrong others had done, we resolutely looked for our own mistakes... We admitted our wrongs honestly...** **STEPS 4 and/or 10 - (Column 4)**	
Where had I been selfish, self-centred or self-seeking?**		
Where had I been dishonest?**		
Where had I been frightened?**		
For what had I been responsible?**		
What decisions did I make based on self that later placed me in a position to be hurt?*		
When in the past did I make this decision? * (Earliest memory)		
Where was I wrong,** what was my part?		

STEPS 6 & 7 – List of Character Defects			

STEP 9 - Amends	STEP 8
	☐ Now ☐ Later ☐ Never

FORMS ONLY

INVENTORY FORMS

Resentment (1) and/or Fear:	The Cause (Column 2)	Affects Our: (Column 3)
Person, Place or Thing		☐ Self-Esteem ☐ Security ☐ Ambitions ☐ Personal Relations ☐ Sex Relations ☐ Pride/Shame ☐ Fear
Ask Ourselves: ** (AA 67.3) * (AA 62.2)	Putting out of our mind the wrong others had done, we resolutely looked for our own mistakes... We admitted our wrongs honestly...** **STEPS 4 and/or 10 - (Column 4)**	
Where had I been selfish, self-centred or self-seeking?**		
Where had I been dishonest?**		
Where had I been frightened?**		
For what had I been responsible?**		
What decisions did I make based on self that later placed me in a position to be hurt?*		
When in the past did I make this decision? * (Earliest memory)		
Where was I wrong,** what was my part?		

STEPS 6 & 7 – List of Character Defects

STEP 9 - Amends	STEP 8
	☐ Now ☐ Later ☐ Never

FOUR COLUMN INVENTORY...

COLUMN WORK

Resentment and/or Fear: (1)	The Cause (Column 2)	Affects Our: (Column 3)
Person, Place or Thing		☐ Self-Esteem ☐ Security ☐ Ambitions ☐ Personal Relations ☐ Sex Relations ☐ Pride/Shame ☐ Fear
Ask Ourselves: ** (AA 67.3) * (AA 62.2)	Putting out of our mind the wrong others had done, we resolutely looked for our own mistakes… We admitted our wrongs honestly…** **STEPS 4 and/or 10 - (Column 4)**	
Where had I been selfish, self-centred or self-seeking?**		
Where had I been dishonest?**		
Where had I been frightened?**		
For what had I been responsible?**		
What decisions did I make based on self that later placed me in a position to be hurt?*		
When in the past did I make this decision? * (Earliest memory)		
Where was I wrong,** what was my part?		
STEPS 6 & 7 – List of Character Defects		

STEP 9 - Amends	STEP 8
	☐ Now ☐ Later ☐ Never

FORMS ONLY

INVENTORY FORMS

Resentment (1) and/or Fear:	The Cause (Column 2)	Affects Our: (Column 3)
Person, Place or Thing		☐ Self-Esteem ☐ Security ☐ Ambitions ☐ Personal Relations ☐ Sex Relations ☐ Pride/Shame ☐ Fear
Ask Ourselves: ** (AA 67.3) * (AA 62.2)	Putting out of our mind the wrong others had done, we resolutely looked for our own mistakes... We admitted our wrongs honestly...** **STEPS 4** and/or **10** - **(Column 4)**	
Where had I been selfish, self-centred or self-seeking?**		
Where had I been dishonest?**		
Where had I been frightened?**		
For what had I been responsible?**		
What decisions did I make based on self that later placed me in a position to be hurt?*		
When in the past did I make this decision? * (Earliest memory)		
Where was I wrong,** what was my part?		
STEPS 6 & 7 – List of Character Defects		
STEP 9 - Amends		**STEP 8**
		☐ Now ☐ Later ☐ Never

FOUR COLUMN INVENTORY...

COLUMN WORK

Resentment (1) and/or Fear:	The Cause (Column 2)	Affects Our: (Column 3)
Person, Place or Thing		☐ Self-Esteem ☐ Security ☐ Ambitions ☐ Personal Relations ☐ Sex Relations ☐ Pride/Shame ☐ Fear
Ask Ourselves: ** (AA 67.3) * (AA 62.2)	Putting out of our mind the wrong others had done, we resolutely looked for our own mistakes... We admitted our wrongs honestly... ** **STEPS 4 and/or 10 - (Column 4)**	
Where had I been selfish, self-centred or self-seeking?**		
Where had I been dishonest?**		
Where had I been frightened?**		
For what had I been responsible?**		
What decisions did I make based on self that later placed me in a position to be hurt?*		
When in the past did I make this decision? * (Earliest memory)		
Where was I wrong,** what was my part?		
STEPS 6 & 7 – List of Character Defects		

STEP 9 - Amends	STEP 8
	☐ Now ☐ Later ☐ Never

FORMS ONLY

INVENTORY FORMS

Resentment (1) and/or Fear:	The Cause (Column 2)	Affects Our: (Column 3)
Person, Place or Thing		☐ Self-Esteem ☐ Security ☐ Ambitions ☐ Personal Relations ☐ Sex Relations ☐ Pride/Shame ☐ Fear
Ask Ourselves: ** (AA 67.3) * (AA 62.2)	Putting out of our mind the wrong others had done, we resolutely looked for our own mistakes… We admitted our wrongs honestly…** **STEPS 4** and/or **10** - **(Column 4)**	
Where had I been selfish, self-centred or self-seeking?**		
Where had I been dishonest?**		
Where had I been frightened?**		
For what had I been responsible?**		
What decisions did I make based on self that later placed me in a position to be hurt?*		
When in the past did I make this decision? * (Earliest memory)		
Where was I wrong,** what was my part?		
STEPS 6 & 7 – List of Character Defects		
STEP 9 - Amends		**STEP 8**
		☐ Now ☐ Later ☐ Never

COLUMN WORK

Resentment (1) and/or Fear:	The Cause (Column 2)	Affects Our: (Column 3)
Person, Place or Thing		☐ Self-Esteem ☐ Security ☐ Ambitions ☐ Personal Relations ☐ Sex Relations ☐ Pride/Shame ☐ Fear
Ask Ourselves: ** (AA 67.3) * (AA 62.2)	Putting out of our mind the wrong others had done, we resolutely looked for our own mistakes… We admitted our wrongs honestly…** **STEPS 4** and/or **10 - (Column 4)**	
Where had I been selfish, self-centred or self-seeking?**		
Where had I been dishonest?**		
Where had I been frightened?**		
For what had I been responsible?**		
What decisions did I make based on self that later placed me in a position to be hurt?*		
When in the past did I make this decision? * (Earliest memory)		
Where was I wrong,** what was my part?		

STEPS 6 & 7 – List of Character Defects				

STEP 9 - Amends	STEP 8
	☐ Now ☐ Later ☐ Never

INVENTORY FORMS

Resentment (1) and/or Fear:	The Cause (Column 2)	Affects Our: (Column 3)
Person, Place or Thing		☐ Self-Esteem ☐ Security ☐ Ambitions ☐ Personal Relations ☐ Sex Relations ☐ Pride/Shame ☐ Fear
Ask Ourselves: ** (AA 67.3) * (AA 62.2)	Putting out of our mind the wrong others had done, we resolutely looked for our own mistakes... We admitted our wrongs honestly...** **STEPS 4** and/or **10 - (Column 4)**	
Where had I been selfish, self-centred or self-seeking?**		
Where had I been dishonest?**		
Where had I been frightened?**		
For what had I been responsible?**		
What decisions did I make based on self that later placed me in a position to be hurt?*		
When in the past did I make this decision? * (Earliest memory)		
Where was I wrong,** what was my part?		
STEPS 6 & 7 – List of Character Defects		
STEP 9 - Amends		**STEP 8**
		☐ Now ☐ Later ☐ Never

COLUMN WORK

Resentment (1) and/or Fear:	The Cause (Column 2)	Affects Our: (Column 3)
Person, Place or Thing		☐ Self-Esteem ☐ Security ☐ Ambitions ☐ Personal Relations ☐ Sex Relations ☐ Pride/Shame ☐ Fear
Ask Ourselves: ** (AA 67.3) * (AA 62.2)	Putting out of our mind the wrong others had done, we resolutely looked for our own mistakes... We admitted our wrongs honestly... ** **STEPS 4 and/or 10 - (Column 4)**	
Where had I been selfish, self-centred or self-seeking?**		
Where had I been dishonest?**		
Where had I been frightened?**		
For what had I been responsible?**		
What decisions did I make based on self that later placed me in a position to be hurt?*		
When in the past did I make this decision? * (Earliest memory)		
Where was I wrong,** what was my part?		

STEPS 6 & 7 – List of Character Defects				

STEP 9 - Amends	STEP 8
	☐ Now ☐ Later ☐ Never

INVENTORY FORMS

Resentment (1) and/or Fear:	The Cause (Column 2)	Affects Our: (Column 3)
Person, Place or Thing		☐ Self-Esteem ☐ Security ☐ Ambitions ☐ Personal Relations ☐ Sex Relations ☐ Pride/Shame ☐ Fear
Ask Ourselves: ** (AA 67.3) * (AA 62.2)	Putting out of our mind the wrong others had done, we resolutely looked for our own mistakes... We admitted our wrongs honestly...** **STEPS 4 and/or 10 - (Column 4)**	
Where had I been selfish, self-centred or self-seeking?**		
Where had I been dishonest?**		
Where had I been frightened?**		
For what had I been responsible?**		
What decisions did I make based on self that later placed me in a position to be hurt?*		
When in the past did I make this decision? * (Earliest memory)		
Where was I wrong,** what was my part?		
STEPS 6 & 7 – List of Character Defects		
STEP 9 - Amends		**STEP 8**
		☐ Now ☐ Later ☐ Never

FOUR COLUMN INVENTORY...

COLUMN WORK

Resentment (1) and/or Fear:	The Cause (Column 2)	Affects Our: (Column 3)
Person, Place or Thing		☐ Self-Esteem ☐ Security ☐ Ambitions ☐ Personal Relations ☐ Sex Relations ☐ Pride/Shame ☐ Fear
Ask Ourselves: ** (AA 67.3) * (AA 62.2)	Putting out of our mind the wrong others had done, we resolutely looked for our own mistakes... We admitted our wrongs honestly...** **STEPS 4 and/or 10 - (Column 4)**	
Where had I been selfish, self-centred or self-seeking?**		
Where had I been dishonest?**		
Where had I been frightened?**		
For what had I been responsible?**		
What decisions did I make based on self that later placed me in a position to be hurt?*		
When in the past did I make this decision? * (Earliest memory)		
Where was I wrong,** what was my part?		
STEPS 6 & 7 – List of Character Defects		

STEP 9 - Amends		STEP 8
		☐ Now ☐ Later ☐ Never

FORMS ONLY

INVENTORY FORMS

Resentment (1) and/or Fear:	The Cause (Column 2)	Affects Our: (Column 3)
Person, Place or Thing		☐ Self-Esteem ☐ Security ☐ Ambitions ☐ Personal Relations ☐ Sex Relations ☐ Pride/Shame ☐ Fear
Ask Ourselves: ** (AA 67.3) * (AA 62.2)	Putting out of our mind the wrong others had done, we resolutely looked for our own mistakes... We admitted our wrongs honestly...** **STEPS 4** and/or **10** - **(Column 4)**	
Where had I been selfish, self-centred or self-seeking?**		
Where had I been dishonest?**		
Where had I been frightened?**		
For what had I been responsible?**		
What decisions did I make based on self that later placed me in a position to be hurt?*		
When in the past did I make this decision? * (Earliest memory)		
Where was I wrong,** what was my part?		

STEPS 6 & 7 – List of Character Defects			

STEP 9 - Amends	STEP 8
	☐ Now ☐ Later ☐ Never

FOUR COLUMN INVENTORY...

COLUMN WORK

Resentment (1) and/or Fear:	The Cause (Column 2)	Affects Our: (Column 3)
Person, Place or Thing		☐ Self-Esteem ☐ Security ☐ Ambitions ☐ Personal Relations ☐ Sex Relations ☐ Pride/Shame ☐ Fear
Ask Ourselves: ** (AA 67.3) * (AA 62.2)	Putting out of our mind the wrong others had done, we resolutely looked for our own mistakes… We admitted our wrongs honestly…** **STEPS 4** and/or **10** - **(Column 4)**	
Where had I been selfish, self-centred or self-seeking?**		
Where had I been dishonest?**		
Where had I been frightened?**		
For what had I been responsible?**		
What decisions did I make based on self that later placed me in a position to be hurt?*		
When in the past did I make this decision? * (Earliest memory)		
Where was I wrong,** what was my part?		

STEPS 6 & 7 – List of Character Defects				

STEP 9 - Amends	STEP 8
	☐ Now ☐ Later ☐ Never

FORMS ONLY

INVENTORY FORMS

Resentment (1) and/or Fear:	The Cause (Column 2)	Affects Our: (Column 3)
Person, Place or Thing		☐ Self-Esteem ☐ Security ☐ Ambitions ☐ Personal Relations ☐ Sex Relations ☐ Pride/Shame ☐ Fear
Ask Ourselves: ** (AA 67.3) * (AA 62.2)	Putting out of our mind the wrong others had done, we resolutely looked for our own mistakes... We admitted our wrongs honestly...** **STEPS 4** and/or **10 - (Column 4)**	
Where had I been selfish, self-centred or self-seeking?**		
Where had I been dishonest?**		
Where had I been frightened?**		
For what had I been responsible?**		
What decisions did I make based on self that later placed me in a position to be hurt?*		
When in the past did I make this decision? * (Earliest memory)		
Where was I wrong,** what was my part?		
STEPS 6 & 7 – List of Character Defects		
STEP 9 - Amends		**STEP 8**
		☐ Now ☐ Later ☐ Never

312   FOUR COLUMN INVENTORY...

COLUMN WORK

Resentment (1) and/or Fear:	The Cause (Column 2)	Affects Our: (Column 3)
Person, Place or Thing		☐ Self-Esteem ☐ Security ☐ Ambitions ☐ Personal Relations ☐ Sex Relations ☐ Pride/Shame ☐ Fear
Ask Ourselves: ** (AA 67.3) * (AA 62.2)	Putting out of our mind the wrong others had done, we resolutely looked for our own mistakes… We admitted our wrongs honestly…** **STEPS 4 and/or 10 - (Column 4)**	
Where had I been selfish, self-centred or self-seeking?**		
Where had I been dishonest?**		
Where had I been frightened?**		
For what had I been responsible?**		
What decisions did I make based on self that later placed me in a position to be hurt?*		
When in the past did I make this decision? * (Earliest memory)		
Where was I wrong,** what was my part?		
STEPS 6 & 7 – List of Character Defects		

STEP 9 - Amends		STEP 8
		☐ Now ☐ Later ☐ Never

FORMS ONLY

INVENTORY FORMS

Resentment (1) and/or Fear:	The Cause (Column 2)	Affects Our: (Column 3)
Person, Place or Thing		☐ Self-Esteem ☐ Security ☐ Ambitions ☐ Personal Relations ☐ Sex Relations ☐ Pride/Shame ☐ Fear
Ask Ourselves: ** (AA 67.3) * (AA 62.2)	Putting out of our mind the wrong others had done, we resolutely looked for our own mistakes... We admitted our wrongs honestly...** **STEPS 4** and/or **10 - (Column 4)**	
Where had I been selfish, self-centred or self-seeking?**		
Where had I been dishonest?**		
Where had I been frightened?**		
For what had I been responsible?**		
What decisions did I make based on self that later placed me in a position to be hurt?*		
When in the past did I make this decision? * (Earliest memory)		
Where was I wrong,** what was my part?		
STEPS 6 & 7 – List of Character Defects		
STEP 9 - Amends		**STEP 8**
		☐ Now ☐ Later ☐ Never

COLUMN WORK

Resentment (1) and/or Fear:	The Cause (Column 2)	Affects Our: (Column 3)
Person, Place or Thing		☐ Self-Esteem ☐ Security ☐ Ambitions ☐ Personal Relations ☐ Sex Relations ☐ Pride/Shame ☐ Fear
Ask Ourselves: ** (AA 67.3) * (AA 62.2)	Putting out of our mind the wrong others had done, we resolutely looked for our own mistakes... We admitted our wrongs honestly...** **STEPS 4 and/or 10 - (Column 4)**	
Where had I been selfish, self-centred or self-seeking?**		
Where had I been dishonest?**		
Where had I been frightened?**		
For what had I been responsible?**		
What decisions did I make based on self that later placed me in a position to be hurt?*		
When in the past did I make this decision? * (Earliest memory)		
Where was I wrong,** what was my part?		

STEPS 6 & 7 – List of Character Defects				

STEP 9 - Amends	STEP 8
	☐ Now ☐ Later ☐ Never

INVENTORY FORMS

Resentment (1) and/or Fear:	The Cause (Column 2)	Affects Our: (Column 3)
Person, Place or Thing		☐ Self-Esteem ☐ Security ☐ Ambitions ☐ Personal Relations ☐ Sex Relations ☐ Pride/Shame ☐ Fear
Ask Ourselves: ** (AA 67.3) * (AA 62.2)	Putting out of our mind the wrong others had done, we resolutely looked for our own mistakes... We admitted our wrongs honestly...** **STEPS 4** and/or **10** - **(Column 4)**	
Where had I been selfish, self-centred or self-seeking?**		
Where had I been dishonest?**		
Where had I been frightened?**		
For what had I been responsible?**		
What decisions did I make based on self that later placed me in a position to be hurt?*		
When in the past did I make this decision? * (Earliest memory)		
Where was I wrong,** what was my part?		

STEPS 6 & 7 – List of Character Defects			

STEP 9 - Amends	STEP 8
	☐ Now ☐ Later ☐ Never

FOUR COLUMN INVENTORY...

COLUMN WORK

Resentment and/or Fear: (1)	The Cause (Column 2)	Affects Our: (Column 3)
Person, Place or Thing		☐ Self-Esteem ☐ Security ☐ Ambitions ☐ Personal Relations ☐ Sex Relations ☐ Pride/Shame ☐ Fear
Ask Ourselves: ** (AA 67.3) * (AA 62.2)	Putting out of our mind the wrong others had done, we resolutely looked for our own mistakes… We admitted our wrongs honestly…** **STEPS 4** and/or **10** - **(Column 4)**	
Where had I been selfish, self-centred or self-seeking?**		
Where had I been dishonest?**		
Where had I been frightened?**		
For what had I been responsible?**		
What decisions did I make based on self that later placed me in a position to be hurt?*		
When in the past did I make this decision? * (Earliest memory)		
Where was I wrong,** what was my part?		

STEPS 6 & 7 – List of Character Defects				

STEP 9 - Amends	STEP 8
	☐ Now ☐ Later ☐ Never

INVENTORY FORMS

Resentment (1) and/or Fear:	The Cause (Column 2)	Affects Our: (Column 3)
Person, Place or Thing		☐ Self-Esteem ☐ Security ☐ Ambitions ☐ Personal Relations ☐ Sex Relations ☐ Pride/Shame ☐ Fear
Ask Ourselves: ** (AA 67.3) * (AA 62.2)	Putting out of our mind the wrong others had done, we resolutely looked for our own mistakes... We admitted our wrongs honestly...** **STEPS 4** and/or **10 - (Column 4)**	
Where had I been selfish, self-centred or self-seeking?**		
Where had I been dishonest?**		
Where had I been frightened?**		
For what had I been responsible?**		
What decisions did I make based on self that later placed me in a position to be hurt?*		
When in the past did I make this decision? * (Earliest memory)		
Where was I wrong,** what was my part?		
STEPS 6 & 7 – List of Character Defects		
STEP 9 - Amends		**STEP 8**
		☐ Now ☐ Later ☐ Never

FOUR COLUMN INVENTORY...

COLUMN WORK

Resentment (1) and/or Fear:	The Cause (Column 2)	Affects Our: (Column 3)
Person, Place or Thing		☐ Self-Esteem ☐ Security ☐ Ambitions ☐ Personal Relations ☐ Sex Relations ☐ Pride/Shame ☐ Fear
Ask Ourselves: ** (AA 67.3) * (AA 62.2)	Putting out of our mind the wrong others had done, we resolutely looked for our own mistakes… We admitted our wrongs honestly…** **STEPS 4 and/or 10 - (Column 4)**	
Where had I been selfish, self-centred or self-seeking?**		
Where had I been dishonest?**		
Where had I been frightened?**		
For what had I been responsible?**		
What decisions did I make based on self that later placed me in a position to be hurt?*		
When in the past did I make this decision? * (Earliest memory)		
Where was I wrong,** what was my part?		

STEPS 6 & 7 – List of Character Defects				

STEP 9 - Amends	STEP 8
	☐ Now ☐ Later ☐ Never

FORMS ONLY

INVENTORY FORMS

Resentment (1) and/or Fear:	The Cause (Column 2)	Affects Our: (Column 3)
Person, Place or Thing		☐ Self-Esteem ☐ Security ☐ Ambitions ☐ Personal Relations ☐ Sex Relations ☐ Pride/Shame ☐ Fear
Ask Ourselves: ** (AA 67.3) * (AA 62.2)	Putting out of our mind the wrong others had done, we resolutely looked for our own mistakes... We admitted our wrongs honestly...** **STEPS 4** and/or **10** - **(Column 4)**	
Where had I been selfish, self-centred or self-seeking?**		
Where had I been dishonest?**		
Where had I been frightened?**		
For what had I been responsible?**		
What decisions did I make based on self that later placed me in a position to be hurt?*		
When in the past did I make this decision? * (Earliest memory)		
Where was I wrong,** what was my part?		

STEPS 6 & 7 – List of Character Defects				

STEP 9 - Amends	STEP 8
	☐ Now ☐ Later ☐ Never

COLUMN WORK

Resentment (1) and/or Fear:	The Cause (Column 2)	Affects Our: (Column 3)
Person, Place or Thing		☐ Self-Esteem ☐ Security ☐ Ambitions ☐ Personal Relations ☐ Sex Relations ☐ Pride/Shame ☐ Fear
Ask Ourselves: ** (AA 67.3) * (AA 62.2)	Putting out of our mind the wrong others had done, we resolutely looked for our own mistakes... We admitted our wrongs honestly...** STEPS 4 and/or 10 - (Column 4)	
Where had I been selfish, self-centred or self-seeking?**		
Where had I been dishonest?**		
Where had I been frightened?**		
For what had I been responsible?**		
What decisions did I make based on self that later placed me in a position to be hurt?*		
When in the past did I make this decision? * (Earliest memory)		
Where was I wrong,** what was my part?		

STEPS 6 & 7 – List of Character Defects

STEP 9 - Amends

	STEP 8
	☐ Now ☐ Later ☐ Never

FORMS ONLY

INVENTORY FORMS

Resentment (1) and/or Fear:	The Cause (Column 2)	Affects Our: (Column 3)
Person, Place or Thing		☐ Self-Esteem ☐ Security ☐ Ambitions ☐ Personal Relations ☐ Sex Relations ☐ Pride/Shame ☐ Fear
Ask Ourselves: ** (AA 67.3) * (AA 62.2)	Putting out of our mind the wrong others had done, we resolutely looked for our own mistakes... We admitted our wrongs honestly...** **STEPS 4** and/or **10** - **(Column 4)**	
Where had I been selfish, self-centred or self-seeking?**		
Where had I been dishonest?**		
Where had I been frightened?**		
For what had I been responsible?**		
What decisions did I make based on self that later placed me in a position to be hurt?*		
When in the past did I make this decision? * (Earliest memory)		
Where was I wrong,** what was my part?		
STEPS 6 & 7 – List of Character Defects		
STEP 9 - Amends		**STEP 8**
		☐ Now ☐ Later ☐ Never

322   FOUR COLUMN INVENTORY...

COLUMN WORK

Resentment (1) and/or Fear:	The Cause (Column 2)	Affects Our: (Column 3)
Person, Place or Thing		☐ Self-Esteem ☐ Security ☐ Ambitions ☐ Personal Relations ☐ Sex Relations ☐ Pride/Shame ☐ Fear
Ask Ourselves: ** (AA 67.3) * (AA 62.2)	Putting out of our mind the wrong others had done, we resolutely looked for our own mistakes… We admitted our wrongs honestly…** **STEPS 4** and/or **10** - **(Column 4)**	
Where had I been selfish, self-centred or self-seeking?**		
Where had I been dishonest?**		
Where had I been frightened?**		
For what had I been responsible?**		
What decisions did I make based on self that later placed me in a position to be hurt?*		
When in the past did I make this decision? * (Earliest memory)		
Where was I wrong,** what was my part?		

STEPS 6 & 7 – List of Character Defects

STEP 9 - Amends

	STEP 8
	☐ Now ☐ Later ☐ Never

FORMS ONLY

INVENTORY FORMS

Resentment (1) and/or Fear:	The Cause (Column 2)	Affects Our: (Column 3)
Person, Place or Thing		☐ Self-Esteem ☐ Security ☐ Ambitions ☐ Personal Relations ☐ Sex Relations ☐ Pride/Shame ☐ Fear
Ask Ourselves: ** (AA 67.3) * (AA 62.2)	Putting out of our mind the wrong others had done, we resolutely looked for our own mistakes... We admitted our wrongs honestly...** **STEPS 4** and/or **10** - **(Column 4)**	
Where had I been selfish, self-centred or self-seeking?**		
Where had I been dishonest?**		
Where had I been frightened?**		
For what had I been responsible?**		
What decisions did I make based on self that later placed me in a position to be hurt?*		
When in the past did I make this decision? * (Earliest memory)		
Where was I wrong,** what was my part?		

STEPS 6 & 7 – List of Character Defects			

STEP 9 - Amends	STEP 8
	☐ Now ☐ Later ☐ Never

FOUR COLUMN INVENTORY...

COLUMN WORK

Resentment (1) and/or Fear:	The Cause (Column 2)	Affects Our: (Column 3)
Person, Place or Thing		☐ Self-Esteem ☐ Security ☐ Ambitions ☐ Personal Relations ☐ Sex Relations ☐ Pride/Shame ☐ Fear
Ask Ourselves: ** (AA 67.3) * (AA 62.2)	Putting out of our mind the wrong others had done, we resolutely looked for our own mistakes... We admitted our wrongs honestly...** **STEPS 4 and/or 10 - (Column 4)**	
Where had I been selfish, self-centred or self-seeking?**		
Where had I been dishonest?**		
Where had I been frightened?**		
For what had I been responsible?**		
What decisions did I make based on self that later placed me in a position to be hurt?*		
When in the past did I make this decision? * (Earliest memory)		
Where was I wrong,** what was my part?		
STEPS 6 & 7 – List of Character Defects			

STEP 9 - Amends	STEP 8
	☐ Now ☐ Later ☐ Never

INVENTORY FORMS

Resentment (1) and/or Fear:	The Cause (Column 2)	Affects Our: (Column 3)
Person, Place or Thing		☐ Self-Esteem ☐ Security ☐ Ambitions ☐ Personal Relations ☐ Sex Relations ☐ Pride/Shame ☐ Fear
Ask Ourselves: ** (AA 67.3) * (AA 62.2)	Putting out of our mind the wrong others had done, we resolutely looked for our own mistakes… We admitted our wrongs honestly…** **STEPS 4 and/or 10 - (Column 4)**	
Where had I been selfish, self-centred or self-seeking?**		
Where had I been dishonest?**		
Where had I been frightened?**		
For what had I been responsible?**		
What decisions did I make based on self that later placed me in a position to be hurt?*		
When in the past did I make this decision? * (Earliest memory)		
Where was I wrong,** what was my part?		

STEPS 6 & 7 – List of Character Defects				

STEP 9 - Amends		STEP 8
		☐ Now ☐ Later ☐ Never

FOUR COLUMN INVENTORY…

COLUMN WORK

Resentment (1) and/or Fear:	The Cause (Column 2)	Affects Our: (Column 3)
Person, Place or Thing		☐ Self-Esteem ☐ Security ☐ Ambitions ☐ Personal Relations ☐ Sex Relations ☐ Pride/Shame ☐ Fear
Ask Ourselves: ** (AA 67.3) * (AA 62.2)	Putting out of our mind the wrong others had done, we resolutely looked for our own mistakes... We admitted our wrongs honestly... ** **STEPS 4 and/or 10 - (Column 4)**	
Where had I been selfish, self-centred or self-seeking?**		
Where had I been dishonest?**		
Where had I been frightened?**		
For what had I been responsible?**		
What decisions did I make based on self that later placed me in a position to be hurt?*		
When in the past did I make this decision? * (Earliest memory)		
Where was I wrong,** what was my part?		

STEPS 6 & 7 – List of Character Defects				

STEP 9 - Amends	STEP 8
	☐ Now ☐ Later ☐ Never

INVENTORY FORMS

Resentment (1) and/or Fear:	The Cause (Column 2)	Affects Our: (Column 3)
Person, Place or Thing		☐ Self-Esteem ☐ Security ☐ Ambitions ☐ Personal Relations ☐ Sex Relations ☐ Pride/Shame ☐ Fear
Ask Ourselves: ** (AA 67.3) * (AA 62.2)	Putting out of our mind the wrong others had done, we resolutely looked for our own mistakes… We admitted our wrongs honestly…** **STEPS 4 and/or 10 - (Column 4)**	
Where had I been selfish, self-centred or self-seeking?**		
Where had I been dishonest?**		
Where had I been frightened?**		
For what had I been responsible?**		
What decisions did I make based on self that later placed me in a position to be hurt?*		
When in the past did I make this decision? * (Earliest memory)		
Where was I wrong,** what was my part?		
STEPS 6 & 7 – List of Character Defects		
STEP 9 - Amends		**STEP 8**
		☐ Now ☐ Later ☐ Never

FOUR COLUMN INVENTORY…

Chapter 3

The Principles

THE PRINCIPLES OF THE PROGRAM

The following are *"the Principles by which AA members recover"* [13] as we see them.

"AA's Twelve Steps are a group of principles, spiritual in nature, which, if practised as a way of life, can expel the obsession to drink (or, we believe, any obsession) *and enable the sufferer to become happily and usefully whole."* [14] *"The basic principles of AA, as they are known today, were borrowed mainly from the fields of religion and medicine."* [15]

When AA began there were six principles. Today, now that we have Twelve Steps, we believe there are twelve principles. *"We begin to see that the AA principles are good ones. Though we are still beset with much rebellion, we increase the practice of these principles out of a sense of responsibility to ourselves, our families, and our groups."* [16] These principles are the *"common denominators of all religions...potent enough to change the lives of men and women.* [17] It is nearly impossible to put these powerful principles created by the Steps into single words, but here is an attempt to do so.

The initial six comprised: **Defeat** (now our Step One); **Honest** self-survey (now our Step Four); **Confession** (now our Step Five); **Restitution** (now our Step Nine); **Conscious contact** with a Higher Power (now our Step Eleven) and **Service** (now our Step Twelve). These principles went with the original Six Steps. We consider the additional principles to be: **Open-mindedness** (Step Two); **Surrender,** (Step Three); **Willingness** (Step Six); **Humility** (Step Seven); **Forgiveness** (Step Eight); **Stewardship** (Step Ten).

THE PRINCIPLES OF THE PROGRAM

1) **Defeat** (Step 1)
Here the acceptance of our powerlessness and the knowledge of our **defeat** are paramount. I cannot make it on my own. "We" begin a life-long process. **Ego deflation** is the removal of a belief in separation. We are not alone or separate. We must be clear that *"any life run on self is not worth living."*

2) **Open Mindedness** (Step 2)
Step Two is the smallest beginning of a pattern of faith *and* **open-mindedness** that builds. First is *faith* in the program, where we see *a power greater than ourselves* at work. To be **O**pen Minded is the **KEY**.

3) **Surrender** (Step 3)
When we walk through the doors of our first meeting, or even with our first call for help, something begins to happen. That "something" becomes clearer by the time of our decision in Step Three. We decided to **surrender** to, and *trust* in, the process of the Steps, *a power greater than ourselves*. The bottom line for **surrender** is the recognition that "I could be wrong."

4) **Honesty** (Step 4)
It can be argued that each of these "Principles" is buried in all the steps; "**Honesty**" is the **KEY**. However, Step Four begins a lifetime of **honest self-survey**.

5) **Confession** (Step 5)
Our AA journey begins with the *courage* to ask for help. For some of us this journey begins with our first meeting. For others of us when we ask for help from a sponsor, but certainly for all of us that *courage* is there by the time we begin the **confession** of our "short comings" in Step Five.

6) **Willingness** (Step 6)
All our answers are found deep inside, **Willingness** is the **KEY**. We must be willing to go against the demands of our self-will to use the tools we have created to, we think, survive; our defects of character.

7) **Humility** (Step 7)
Step 7 reminds us to give up our attempts at fixing ourselves and turn it over to God, an act of **humility** and open-mindedness that most of us never understood.

8) **Forgiveness** (Step 8)
Forgiveness begins here when we release resentments and hurts, "real or imagined," becoming ready to make amends.

9) **Restitution** (Step 9)
Amend, means "to mend" our past behaviour. Our new found life long experience of "mending" and making **restitution** for our past (and not so past) actions begins on Step Nine. This is where the "promises" are received, giving us an experience of **freedom** never before experienced.

10) **Stewardship** (Steps 10)
The so-called "maintenance steps" of the program begin with Step 10, teaching us perseverance and **stewardship**. *Perseverance* is just plain "keep on, keeping on," where as **stewardship** is the learning of the necessity for daily maintenance of the "Promises." Dr. Bob said that *"We are stewards of what we have."* [18]

11) **Conscious Contact** (Step 11)
Now that we have a belief in a Higher Power we *"improve our conscious contact"* with that Power greater than ourselves through Prayer and meditation. This is where we find a wonderful source of **Conscious** enlightenment. Enlightenment can only come to a **conscious** mind. A greater **conscious contact** is the benefit of the *patient* use of daily prayer and meditation, as we give up our desire for instant gratification. We must "Let Go and Let God". We become more **conscious** of our beliefs, of our actions, and attitudes. And most importantly we become more and more God **conscious**, "a spiritual awakening."

12) **Service** (Step 12)
Our entire life, through the *"practice of these principles in all our affairs"* [19] becomes one of service, including our jobs, and our home life, everywhere. We learn the true meaning of the word *charity*, as we carry the message through **service** and become a beacon to others in AA. In Step Twelve it is made clear that we must "give it away to keep it*"*. *"Our real purpose is to fit ourselves to be of maximum service to God and the people about us."* [20]

The References

REFERENCES

The page number is before the decimal and paragraph number after.

---

[1] Best of the Grapevine – Page(s) – 128.2
[2] Experience, Strength, & Hope – Page(s) 40.3, 41.1
[3] Experience, Strength, & Hope – Page(s) 335.3
[4] Experience, Strength, & Hope – Page(s) 332.1
[5] Experience, Strength, & Hope – Page(s) 213.1
[6] Twelve Steps and Twelve Traditions – Page 53.4 – British Edition
[7] Experience, Strength, & Hope – Page(s) 330.3
[8] Experience, Strength, & Hope – Page(s) 214.2
[9] Think and Grow Rich – Napoleon Hill
[10] Alcoholics Anonymous – Page 62.2
[11] Twelve Steps and Twelve Traditions – Page 127.2 – British Edition
[12] DR. BOB and the Good Oldtimers – Page 158.2
[13] Twelve Steps and Twelve Traditions – Page 15.2 – British Edition
[14] Twelve Steps and Twelve Traditions – Page 15.3 – British Edition
[15] Twelve Steps and Twelve Traditions – British Edition – Page 16.4
[16] Language of the Heart – Page 302.2
[17] Pass It On—Bill Wilson and the AA Message – Page 128.1
[18] DR. BOB and the Good Oldtimers – Page 105.1
[19] Alcoholics Anonymous Page 60.1
[20] Alcoholics Anonymous – Page 77.1

REFERENCES

Also available from *HP* Publishing:

Meditation CDs	**USA**	**UK**
– Prayer of St Francis of Assisi	$ 16.95	£ 7.95
– Forgiveness Meditation – (available soon)	$ 16.95	£ 7.95
– Life's an Ocean – (available soon)	$ 16.95	£ 7.95
Books		
– Deep Soul Cleansing (text) Hardcover	$ 43.95	£ 22.50
– Deep Soul Cleansing (text) Paperback	$ 26.95	£ 13.95
– Deep Soul Cleansing – Workbook	$ 44.50	£ 22.95
– Maintaining the Promises – Daily Hardcover	$ 55.95	£ 27.95
– Maintaining the Promises – Daily Paperback	$ 32.95	£ 19.50
– 366 Daily Prayers – Paperback	$ 24.95	£ 12.50
– Four Column Inventory Forms Only Paperback	$ 28.95	£ 14.50

Write for more information about upcoming Retreats and/or Workshops or send your order to:

United Kingdom

HP Retreats

63 Shepherds Court
LONDON England
W12-8PW
44+(0)208-740-8567
www.hpretreats.org

United States

HP Publishing

1701 The Greensway
Building 1425
Jacksonville Beach FL 32250
1+ 904-543-0608
www.hppublishing.com

Orders are best made via the internet do to our busy travel schedule.

MAINTAINING THE PROMISES...DAILY

www.ingramcontent.com/pod-product-compliance
Lightning Source LLC
Chambersburg PA
CBHW032000220426
43664CB00005B/90